Holy SH** Sherlock!

You're retired, now what?

Holy SH** Sherlock!

You're retired, now what?

A Baby Boomers' Guide to Happily
Ever After

By

B.A. GINTHER

Disclaimer

This publication is designed to provide accurate and timely information with regard to the subject matters included all of which is based upon personal observations, opinions (author and other retirees) and research available at the time of writing. It is not intended to render or replace legal, accounting, medical, psychological or other professional services. If legal, accounting, medical, psychological or other professional services are required, the services of a competent professional person should be sought. It is the intention of the author that the resources and information provided will serve as a guide for individuals who are or soon will be retiring. Although the author and publisher have made every effort to ensure that the information in this book was correct at press time, the author and publisher do not assume and hereby disclaim any liability to any party for any loss, damage, or disruption caused by errors or omissions, whether such errors or omissions result from negligence, accident, or any other cause.

In addition this publication includes numerous stories and jokes that are intended to provide light-hearted entertainment. There is no intention to perpetuate any stereotypes or to single out any group or individual. The original authors of the jokes are unknown except where credit is given. The author and publisher do not assume and hereby disclaim any liability to any party for any loss, damage, or disruption caused by errors or omissions, whether such errors or omissions result from negligence, accident, or any other cause.

✩✩✩

Acknowledgements

Writing a book is quite a journey and it would have been impossible to complete without the love and support of many people in my life. My thanks and gratitude to each cannot be measured.

First, I would like to express my deepest appreciation to my husband Myles. You gave me the space and encouragement I needed to persist in seeing this project through to the end. Besides being my greatest champion, you often played the annoying role of "devil's advocate" so about the time I felt comfortable with a thought or position you disrupted that peace with questions and persuaded me to see other perspectives. I hate when that happens, but it was good. When you surprised me with something I hadn't thought about I usually exclaimed, "Holy Sh**, Sherlock, who knew?" You often wondered where I came up with the off-the-wall book title, and now you know. You are a kind, gentle and devoted partner who is the love of my life. Thank you, Myles, for your love and support; I am a better person because of you.

My thanks also to my wonderful family; three daughters (Carolyn, Morgan and Jessica), son-in-law (Sean) and two adorable grandchildren all of whom, for the most part, have no clue what all I am working on at any given time but who encourage and believe in me unconditionally anyway. How could I not be a winner with all of you in my corner? Thank you all for always being there.

A special thanks to my daughter Morgan, sister-in-law Julie E. and cousin Coreen N. for the extra editorial and technical assistance each of you graciously provided for me.

It has been said that it "takes a village to raise a child," which indeed it does, but I would like to suggest that it also takes a "village" to make any worthwhile transition in life. In this case the transition is retirement and I would like to thank my "village" for helping me to document the lessons learned about retiring: My "village" includes all of those who were willing to share the issues, problems and the solutions they encountered when they retired or that they were simply willing to drink a lot of beer and laugh about the circumstances of life: Many thanks to my sister and brother-in-law Nadine and Les S., my husband's aunt and uncle, Marianne and Don B., our wonderful neighbors and fellow "Happy Hour" devotees Helen and Phil R., Noreen and Mid C., Judy and Dale B., and Bonnie and Grant K., our dear friends Sue and George B. and Jackie and George T., the Monday afternoon women's Whine and Cheese group, and last but certainly not least, Barb H. who taught a memoir writing class and all the members of the class (Fran, Penny, Joyce, Tom, Ron and others) where I found support, encouragement, camaraderie and some of the inspiration for this project. Thank you all very much for all of your wisdom, humor and willingness to share the details of your life. You are all very special to me.

✻✻✻

Table of Contents

✫✫✫

Preface

Dear Readers,

On June 15, 2012 I retired, along with thousands of other Baby Boomers who also retired on that particular day in that particular year and a few months later my husband joined the ranks of the retired, too. With this robust trend well underway, the number of boomers who will retire over the next couple of decades is astonishing. The great Baby Boomer passage into retirement began in January of 2011 and will continue at a record pace with approximately ten thousand new retirees every day over each of the next nineteen or twenty years. This means there is the potential for approximately 3,650,000 new retirees every year for the foreseeable future.

If you are a Baby Boomer and, depending upon your age and state of health *when* you retire and how you take care of yourself *after* you retire, you may be looking at a retirement that could last 20 or 30 years. Just think of it, a period of time to be retired that is nearly as long as your entire work career. Add to that the fact that many Baby Boomers are retiring younger and healthier than previous generations and suddenly, navigating the future seems a lot like navigating the past. In the 1960's we boomers first started to make a mark on the world by reimaging and redefining everything we touched and it seems to be happening again as we hit our own mid-60's and are reinventing retirement. However, it is far more than change for change sake, for many of us in the boomer generation everything about retirement looks a lot like a whole new chapter, a second chance or an opportunity for an "encore" performance and a time to make a difference.

Some say that Baby Boomers have not saved enough to last through a long retirement although most continue to retire early in spite of it. Others say a majority of Baby Boomers have, in fact, planned well for the financial part of retirement (some are even retiring wealthier than previous generations); but have paid little attention to preparing for other life changes (physical, social, and emotional) that are an equally big part of the transition to retirement. Obviously there is truth to both statements and without a doubt, having enough money to live the retirement lifestyle you desire is very important, but so is having a vision for your retirement. What exactly is the lifestyle you wish for? How do you prepare for future events or lifestyle adjustments that you do not even know exist? Besides the obvious big change that you will no longer go to work each day, there are many subtle life changes in retirement such as managing togetherness with your spouse. My husband is away from home for a few hours today playing softball. Thank God. It is the first *freaking* 15 minutes I have had all to myself in 6 months and I am so happy to have some "alone time" I don't know whether to sing and dance or just laugh out loud! Instead I decided to write a book! I am joking ---but not really--- too much face time in retirement can be a serious issue especially when you move from being an evening and weekend couple to a 24/7/365 couple. Redefining your relationships in the retirement years is very important and can contribute either positively or negatively to your future health, happiness and, in some cases, possibly your marital status.

This book offers information on a variety of topics related to making a successful transition into retirement and is organized in a way to give the reader some context about why each particular subject is included in the book, followed by a summary of findings and resources to locate additional information. Moreover, each chapter also has a good number of very funny jokes and stories scattered throughout for the reader's laugh out loud enjoyment.

Hopefully you will find value in some of what my husband and I have learned through our experiences during this first year of our retirement plus the lessons gleaned through the collective wisdom of other retirees who continue to nurture and mentor us. It is abundantly clear is that there is much to know about retirement (more than any single book can impart) and each of us can make retiring a little better for all of us if we share what we learn with each other. Retiring isn't just about reaching a destination, but also about enjoying the journey. Enjoy your journey!

Sincerely,

B. A. Ginther

✫✫✫

CHAPTER 1

When You Retire, Every Day is Saturday

In the past year, my husband and I sold our house, downsized, retired from our careers and moved 2000 miles away from our home in major city in the Midwest where we had lived, worked, and raised three children the past 33 years. We moved to a 55+ retirement community near Phoenix, Arizona. Needless to say after 33 years we had our family and many friends and connections to our community and surrounding area so retiring wasn't a "put your feet up and kick back" kind of event for us. There was a lot of work and planning involved with all of the above and, as you might expect, a few unplanned surprises along the way, too.

We knew that retiring was going to be a process, not a single one-time event, and part of it would include making a number of important decisions in the upcoming year including Social Security, Medicare and estate planning. Nevertheless we entered the first months of retirement thinking we were through the worst of it, having successfully completed a cross country move, and we were looking forward to the lifestyle described by our retired friends; *when you are retired, every day is Saturday.* Who needs to get ready for Saturday? We certainly had a notion of what a Saturday was and if that was retirement then we were all in, like four aces in a poker hand.

However, it didn't take long for us to discover that retired life is far more complicated than the *every day is Saturday* analogy suggests and that there is much more to think about and act on in retirement than meets the eye, which brings us to the purpose of this book. Odd as it may sound, the inspiration originally came from the Medicare program! Medicare is very complicated and trying to understand Medicare is very frustrating. I kept saying to myself (and my husband), "This shouldn't be so hard. I am an educated person and fairly familiar with insurance jargon and terminology so why is this so difficult?" As I continued to study the information and options for myself, I began to ask others what they had done or, were doing, to sort it out and nearly everyone expressed that same high level of frustration that I was feeling. Many said they finally gave up and enrolled in whichever plan a trusted friend or relative suggested to them. I persisted in learning about Medicare and while I worked at that, other topics began to emerge naturally in conversations with other retirees at various times and in various groups. The book began to take shape. The information provided is not intended to provide or replace legal, medical, accounting or any other kind of professional advice, but rather to give the reader a "heads up" about some issues that may have an impact on them when they retire. And, just for fun (because retirement is fun), it also contains a considerable number of very humorous jokes and stories.

Why jokes and stories? Well, never once in my life did I ever intend to write a serious book about a serious subject like retirement issues or, for that matter, a serious book about any serious issue. My real passion in life has always been to make people laugh and over the years I have told and retold some of the best jokes ever written and always planned to publish a book of the funniest ones. However, during this past year as the matters of retirement got into my thinking and nagged at me to do something with them instead. I came to believe that the transition to retirement could be much easier for all of us if each of us would share what we learn; to (as they say) *pay it forward.* With that lofty goal in mind I began to gather my thoughts and organize topics and blah, blah, blah, blah, blah… subjects were easy to identify, seemed logical, interesting and would be significant to others thinking about retiring, too, but the manuscript was missing something. Ah, yes, it was missing laughter. Hence this book became a blend of serious topics mingled with lighthearted zany nonsense that is included for only one reason and that is to entertain the reader and bring about laughter. I should, though, make a disclaimer right up front. Some of the jokes and story sections include a few swear words. I personally do not swear all the time, but on occasion a well placed cuss word here or there accentuates a joke or story and gives a particular emphasis and humorous effect and while this is not an R-rated book some of the jokes and stories are definitely PG-13. I am just saying…..in the world of jokes, nothing is sacred. Please don't take offense. There is no intention to perpetuate any stereotypes, be insensitive toward anyone, or to single out any group or individual. What the hell, I didn't write them, I am just retelling them.

My life-long affinity for swearing is actually the fault of my older brother. I grew up in a farming family in a small town in southwestern North Dakota. I had two brothers (one younger and one older) and two sisters (also one younger and one older). I was the middle child (yes, with all the usual emotional baggage that human behavior experts say comes from that family placement) and age-wise I was closest to my older brother. He was the culprit who regularly led me astray.

Our cussing and swearing started one cold winter morning when we were seven and eight years old. My brother decided it was time we learned how to swear and the best way to learn it was to do it, so he whispered, "Just follow me. It will be easy."

We went into the kitchen and mom turned to my brother first and said, "Good morning, son, what would you like for breakfast today?"

Without blinking an eye my brother replied, "Oh hell, I'll have a bowl of Coco Puffs and make it a **damn** big bowl."

Mother grabbed him by the shirt collar and guided him into the next room without his feet ever touching the ground and closed the door. I could hear a lot of talking, spanking and crying going on in there for several minutes.

A little while later mom returned to the kitchen alone. With her hands on her hips she turned to face me and said, "And what will you be having for breakfast this morning?"

I thought for a second and blurted out, "Well you can bet your ass it isn't gonna be Coco Puffs!"

When it came to swearing, I held my tongue for quite some time, after that incident but my brother never did learn his lesson. In December of that same year he got a train set for his birthday and one day our mother was standing in the doorway of the living room watching him play with his new prized toy. Dad had mounted the set on a large piece of plywood so the train methodically chugged around and around the circular track. There was a shrill whistle now and then and an occasional stop where my brother would shout some orders to an imaginary engineer and give a loud call for passengers, "All Aboard!"

He was having a good time and never noticed mom watching when he stopped the train and instructed his make-believe passengers with the following orders: "Okay, all you sons-a-bitches getting off at this stop, get moving and do it fast. Take your belongings from the overhead bins and get the hell off the train. We are running late and don't need to waste any more time on your sorry asses." Still not noticing mother, he continued, "And all you sons-a-bitches who are getting onboard at this stop, get your things stowed and your butts into a seat as damn fast as you can. We need to get this train moving on down the tracks **now**. All Aboard! All Abooooaaaarrrrdddd."

Mother was appalled and after she picked her chin up off the floor, she told my brother our family didn't use language like that and he was done playing with the train for the next two hours. He was sent to his room for punishment, where he was to sit and think about using better words.

Two hours passed and once again you could hear the electric train humming around the track in the living room. Mother paused what she was doing and went over to the doorway to observe once again. My brother stopped the train and he spoke to his imaginary passengers in a low steady voice and said: "Folks, for your safety please remain seated until the train comes to a complete standstill. For those who are departing at this stop we want to thank you for traveling with us today. Please take your time to locate all of your belongings and carefully watch your step as you make your way to the platform below. We trust you had an enjoyable ride, we appreciate your business and sincerely hope you will travel with us again real soon."

In that same cheerful tone my brother went on to say, "And we would like to welcome everyone who is joining us at this stop. We are very happy to have you onboard and urge you to take your time selecting a seat and to make yourself comfortable before the train begins moving. Please let us know if you need our assistance and remember kind folks, we are here to serve you. All Aaaabbbbboooard! Ladies and gentlemen we will be departing the station shortly." "Oh," he added, "and for those of you, who are pissed off about the two hour delay, please see the bitch in the kitchen!"

If you are thinking to yourself, *very funny but am I missing something, what does swearing or toy trains have to do with retirement*? Be assured you are not losing "it" the stories do not have anything to do with retirement, at least not directly, but rather in the case of these stories, the point has to do with laughter. Laughing every day is extremely valuable for living a long and happy retirement. It is right up there with breathing clean air and eating your fruits and vegetables every day. To take a page from Warren Buffet, the successful multi-gazillionaire investor who says his Rule #1 is to never lose money and Rule #2 is to never forget Rule #1. Similarly, in this book Rule #1 is to laugh every day and Rule #2 is to never forget Rule #1. Retirement can be a carefree and playful time in our lives much like when we were children if we can get back into the habit of laughing often. Expect some very funny jokes and stories throughout the forthcoming chapters and go ahead let yourself go, laugh out loud.

Both of the previous stories are old jokes adapted to seem as though they actually happened in my family. They didn't. Not that they couldn't have because my brother and I were the kind of off-the-wall individuals that these fictional characters were and we got into similar scrapes and situations many times all on our own but, hey, it's a book and is going to have some information that is serious and not a laughing matter as well as some stories that were added for the sole purpose of entertainment and to serve as a reminder to always enjoy yourself in life. After this section the jokes and stories will be in light gray shaded areas so that you will easily see them coming and going!

Good luck on planning your retirement and the best times of your life. May every day be like a Saturday!

"Laughing is like food for the soul. In each of us there is a child dying to get out and to be his childlike self." **Dr. Madan Kataria** (founder of *Laughter Yoga Clubs).*

✿✿✿

CHAPTER 2

Laugh Every Day

A low and mellow "Whoooo Whoooo Whoooo," penetrates the dry air and echoes off the houses in a Gold Canyon, Arizona neighborhood. Activity stops and everyone within earshot becomes still for a moment to listen again. It almost sounds like one of the local doves trying to secure its territory, but not quite, the sound is off. It is a lower pitch and the notes hang in the air longer than those of our feathered friends in the vicinity. The call comes a second time, "Whoooo Whoooo Whoooo." Ah, yes, it is four o'clock in the afternoon and our neighbor Mid, is out on his patio making this flute-like sound by blowing across the top of his newly opened bottle of beer. It signals to the neighborhood that "Happy Hour" is about to begin. Our house is one of four that are back-to-back (patio-to-patio) at the end of a block in our 55+ retirement development and action described above happens nearly every day on one of those four patios.

When my husband and I first arrived in Arizona, in June 2012, most days were too hot to spend much time on the patio. Often at midnight it was still 90 or 95 degrees. However, by early September all that changed. Every day was unbelievably beautiful with blue skies stretching from horizon to horizon and the days warmed by brilliant sun shine followed by cool dry bug-free evenings so everyone in the neighborhood enjoyed the late afternoon outdoors. Each neighbor would shout a friendly greeting and wave to the others. It was a bit formal, but in the past when people hosted a "Happy Hour" it usually meant they would prepare snacks and provide beverages. It was the unwritten rule for patio entertaining and involved a little or a lot of work for the host depending upon what all you wanted to serve.

Over a short time the four couples on our end of the block developed a strong friendship with each other and as a group; we addressed the Happy Hour "elephant in the room" with a plan. The first person on their patio sends the Happy Hour signal by blowing across the top of his/her bottle of beer. All of those available and who wish to join that day bring their own beverage of choice and meet the others on that patio. No food or snacks are expected and the "host" provides a second beer, drink or soft drink. Everyone stays one hour and then goes home.

It is a short and sweet sixty minutes filled with laughter as we bait and joke with each other, share our funny stories and adventures, talk about our kids, grandkids and together solve the problems of the world as well as the day-to-day retirement or life issues we all encounter. We laugh at ourselves and with each other. The eight of us have developed good chemistry. Occasionally we take our Happy Hour on the road and go out to dinner together but then, of course, our emphasis is on food rather than drink. Now when it is too hot to be outside in the summer months, we take turns hosting Happy Hour inside around our kitchen tables and on cooler afternoons, we hear the beckoning sound of the beer bottle "Whoooo Whoooo Whoooo!" The location of the "Happy Hour" patio rotates from house to house depending upon who gets outside first in the afternoon. When the laughter fills the air, other neighbors (from farther into the block or across the street) frequently wander over to join the fun and enjoy the camaraderie, too.

Quite often friends and neighbors will say to us that we have the best neighborhood in the development. There is no doubt, we do have a good one, but there are many other great neighborhoods in this development (and everywhere else), too, and I wondered why they felt that way so I asked them. Every single person said it was because they could hear us laughing and having fun.

It has always been very clear to me over my lifetime (both personally and professionally) that laughter is the key to successful relationships; it can diffuse anger or negative emotions and promote good feelings and build trust. I have to admit that even before I began to research the benefits of laughter, I knew that it had great value and now more than ever I believe that (physically and emotionally) people need laughter and laughing every day is extremely important to a long and happy life (retirement)!

Kindergarten Lesson

I once knew a kindergarten teacher who was teaching her students a unit on taste. She had obtained several flavors of Lifesavers candy and blindfolds for each child.

The teacher said, "Students, we are conducting a test today on the sense of taste so first I will ask everyone to put on a blindfold." After the kids had placed the blindfolds over their eyes the teacher handed out the first Lifesaver.

When each child had a Lifesaver the teacher gave her instructions, "When I say 'go,' I want you to place the Lifesaver in your mouth and taste it to see if you can correctly identify the flavor. When you think you know the answer, just shout it out. Is everyone ready?"

The little blindfolded heads bobbed up and down to indicate they were ready.

"Go," said the teacher.

The students quickly placed the Lifesavers in their mouths and noisily began to lick and suck the pieces of candy. In a short time five or six children shouted out, "Cherry, its cherry flavored!"

"You are right, it is cherry flavored. Good job," the teacher acknowledged. "Let's try another one," and this time she handed each child a lemon flavored Lifesaver which they quickly put into their mouths and once again concentrated on the flavor.

This one was a little tougher and it took the students several minutes before a couple of them finally ventured a guess and hollered out, "Lemon, we think it is lemon!"

The teacher was quite pleased and said, "You really know your flavors; let's try one more and this one may be even more difficult than the other two."

Without delay the teacher handed out the next Lifesaver, which was honey flavored. Once again the students rolled the candy around in their mouths and, although it was sweet and delicious, no one could quite identify the flavor. They were stumped.

After several minutes passed the teacher finally said, "Okay, I will give you a little hint. The name of this flavor is a word your mommy and daddy sometimes call each other."

> Suddenly a little boy in the back of the room yelled out, "Whoa! Spit 'em out! They're assholes!"

It is in a gray box, it's a story, it is not true---I never knew a Kindergarten teacher who conducted this experiment. Obviously it was created by some weird bastard who was totally warped by his kindergarten experience and probably made it up. It is pretty funny though and could be true for someone, somewhere. Just not me and hopefully, not you either but it made me laugh the first time I heard it and it still makes me laugh today.

While the story may not be true, one thing that is true is the old adage, "laughter is the best medicine." Decades of scientific research have shown that laughter strengthens your immune system, enhances your energy, lessens pain, and protects you from the damaging effects of stress. Best of all, this valuable commodity is fun, totally free, accessible to everyone 24/7, easy to use and readily available to share with others. A compelling body of evidence has been gathered to support the positive impact that humor and laughter have on your physical, mental, spiritual, and social health and general well-being.

My Stomach Ache

Life just gets better as you get older doesn't it. I was in a Starbucks Coffee recently when my stomach started rumbling and I realized that I desperately needed to fart. The place was packed but the music was really loud so to get relief and reduce embarrassment I timed my farts to the beat of the music. After a couple of songs I started to feel much better. I finished my coffee and noticed that everyone was staring at me. I suddenly remembered that I was listening to my IPod.

This is what happens when old people start using technology.

An excellent place to learn about the benefits of laughter is at the site of a non-profit organization called **Helpguide. org**. It features research-based studies, interesting articles and resources in many life issues categories including abuse, addictions, eating disorders, Post Traumatic Stress Disorder (PTSD), as well as the health benefits of laughter and more. A recent article, "Laughter is the Best Medicine," provides a first rate summary of the health benefits of laughter and is partially reprinted here with permission. Visit **www. helpguide.org** to see the full article and related links. Enter the word *laughter* in the site search box to find additional resources. All rights reserved and remember this material is for information and support only; not a substitute for professional advice.

Laughter is the Best Medicine

The Health Benefits of Humor and Laughter

Humor is infectious. The sound of roaring laughter is far more contagious than any cough, sniffle, or sneeze. When laughter is shared, it binds people together and increases happiness and intimacy. Laughter also triggers healthy physical changes in the body. Humor and laughter strengthen your immune system, boost your energy, diminish pain, and protect you from the damaging effects of stress. Best of all, this priceless medicine is fun, free, and easy to use

Laughter is strong medicine for mind and body

"Your sense of humor is one of the most powerful tools you have to make certain that your daily mood and emotional state support good health."

~ Paul E. McGhee, Ph.D.

Laughter is a powerful antidote to stress, pain, and conflict. Nothing works faster or more dependably to bring your mind and body back into balance than a good laugh. Humor lightens your burdens, inspires hopes, connects you to others, and keeps you grounded, focused, and alert.

With so much power to heal and renew, the ability to laugh easily and frequently is a tremendous resource for surmounting problems, enhancing your relationships, and supporting both physical and emotional health.

Laughter is good for your health

- **Laughter relaxes the whole body.** A good, hearty laugh relieves physical tension and stress, leaving your muscles relaxed for up to 45 minutes.

- **Laughter boosts the immune system.** Laughter decreases stress hormones and increases immune cells and infection-fighting antibodies, thus improving your resistance to disease.

- **Laughter triggers the release of endorphins,** the body's natural feel-good chemicals. Endorphins promote an overall sense of well-being and can even temporarily relieve pain.

- **Laughter protects the heart.** Laughter improves the function of blood vessels and increases blood flow, which can help protect you against a heart attack and other cardiovascular problems.

The Benefits of Laughter

Physical Health Benefits:

- Boosts immunity
- Lowers stress hormones
- Decreases pain
- Relaxes your muscles
- Prevents heart disease

Mental Health Benefits:

- Adds joy and zest to life
- Eases anxiety and fear
- Relieves stress
- Improves mood
- Enhances resilience

Social Benefits:

- Strengthens relationships
- Attracts others to us
- Enhances teamwork
- Helps defuse conflict
- Promotes group bonding

Laughter and humor help you stay emotionally healthy

Laughter makes you feel good. And the good feeling that you get when you laugh remains with you even after the laughter subsides. Humor helps you keep a positive, optimistic outlook through difficult situations, disappointments, and loss.

More than just a respite from sadness and pain, laughter gives you the courage and strength to find new sources of meaning and hope. Even in the most difficult of times, a laugh–or even simply a smile–can go a long way toward making you feel better. And laughter really is contagious—just hearing laughter primes your brain and readies you to smile and join in the fun.

The link between laughter and mental health

- **Laughter dissolves distressing emotions.** You can't feel anxious, angry, or sad when you're laughing.

- **Laughter helps you relax and recharge.** It reduces stress and increases energy, enabling you to stay focused and accomplish more.

- **Humor shifts perspective**, allowing you to see situations in a more realistic, less threatening light. A humorous perspective creates psychological distance, which can help you avoid feeling overwhelmed.

The social benefits of humor and laughter

Humor and playful communication strengthen our relationships by triggering positive feelings and fostering emotional connection. When we laugh with one another, a positive bond is created. This bond acts as a strong buffer against stress, disagreements, and disappointment.

Laughing with others is more powerful than laughing alone

Shared laughter is one of the most effective tools for keeping relationships fresh and exciting. All emotional sharing builds strong and lasting relationship bonds, but sharing laughter and play also adds joy, vitality, and resilience. And humor is a powerful and effective way to heal resentments, disagreements, and hurts. Laughter unites people during difficult times.

Incorporating more humor and play into your daily interactions can improve the quality of your love relationships— as well as your connections with co-workers, family members, and friends. Using humor and laughter in relationships allows you to:

- **Be more spontaneous.** Humor gets you out of your head and away from your troubles.

- **Let go of defensiveness.** Laughter helps you forget judgments, criticisms, and doubts.

- **Release inhibitions.** Your fear of holding back and holding on are set aside.

Ways to help yourself see the lighter side of life:

- **Laugh at yourself.** Share your embarrassing moments. The best way to take yourself less seriously is to talk about times when you took yourself too seriously.

- **Attempt to laugh at situations rather than bemoan them.** Look for the humor in a bad situation, and uncover the irony and absurdity of life. This will help improve your mood and the mood of those around you.

- **Surround yourself with reminders to lighten up.** Keep a toy on your desk or in your car. Put up a funny poster in your office. Choose a computer screensaver that makes you laugh. Frame photos of you and your family or friends having fun.

- **Keep things in perspective.** Many things in life are beyond your control—particularly the behavior of other people. While you might think taking the weight of the world on your shoulders is admirable, in the long run it's unrealistic, unproductive, unhealthy, and even egotistical.

- **Deal with your stress.** Stress is a major impediment to humor and laughter.

- **Pay attention to children and emulate them.** They are the experts on playing, taking life lightly, and laughing.

Checklist for lightening up

When you find yourself taken over by what seems to be a horrible problem, ask these questions:

- Is it really worth getting upset over?

- Is it worth upsetting others?

- Is it that important?

- Is it that bad?

- Is the situation irreparable?

- Is it really your problem?

Use humor and play to overcome challenges and enhance your life

The ability to laugh, play, and have fun with others not only makes life more enjoyable but also helps you solve problems, connect with others, and be more creative. People who incorporate humor and play into their daily lives find that humor and play renews them and their relationships.

Group Therapy

A psychiatrist was conducting a group therapy session with four young mothers and their small children.

"You all have obsessions," he observed.

To the first mother, Mary, he said, "You are obsessed with eating. You've even named your daughter Candy."

He turned to the second mom, Ann: "Your obsession is with money. Again, it manifests itself in your child's name, Penny."

He turned to the third mom, Joyce: "Your obsession is alcohol. This too shows itself in your child's name, Brandy."

At this point, the fourth mother, Carol, quietly got up, took her little boy by the hand, and whispered, "Come on, Dick, this guy doesn't know what in the hell he's talking about. Let's pick up Peter and little Willy from school and go get dinner."

✲✲✲

Laughter Yoga

A Golf Story

John decided to go golfing in northern Minnesota with his buddy, Keith. So they loaded up John's minivan and headed north. After driving for a few hours, they got caught in a terrible blizzard and they pulled into a nearby farm and asked the attractive lady who answered the door if they could spend the night.

'I realize it's terrible weather out there and I have this huge house all to myself, but I'm recently widowed,' she explained and 'I'm afraid the neighbors will talk if I let you stay in my house.'

'Don't worry,' John said 'We'll be happy to sleep in the barn. And if the weather breaks, we'll be gone at first light.'

The lady agreed, and the two men found their way to the barn and settled in for the night.

Come morning, the weather had cleared, and they got on their way. They enjoyed a great weekend of golf. But about nine months later, John got an unexpected letter from an attorney. It took him a few minutes to figure it out, but he finally determined that it was from the attorney of that attractive widow he had met on the golf weekend. He dropped in on his friend Keith and asked,

'Keith, do you remember that good-looking widow from the farm we stayed at on our golf holiday up North about 9 months ago?' 'Yes, I do.' Said Keith.

'Did you, er, happen to get up in the middle of the night, go up to the house and pay her a visit?'

'Well, um, yes!,' Keith said, a little embarrassed about being found out, 'I have to admit that I did.'

'And did you happen to give her my name instead of telling her your name?'

Keith's face turned beet red and he said,

'Yeah, look, I'm sorry, buddy. I'm afraid I did.'

'Why do you ask?'

'She just died and left me everything.'

Some of us like to tell jokes and funny stories and others of us wilt into a damp pile of polyester and cotton just thinking about getting the punch line right. However, it is important to know that jokes or funny stories are not required to laugh. One can simply engage in the physical act of laughing and receive all of the same benefits of laughing at something that is actually funny. With that in mind a great tool to help you laugh every day is Laughter Yoga.

Laughter Yoga was the brainchild of Dr. Madan Kataria, a physician from Mumbai, India. Dr. Kataria is the advocate and founder of Laughter Clubs worldwide. People who attend laughter club "meetings" laugh for no reason and while doing so learn to combine yogic breathing (Pranayama) with wholehearted laughter. The physical act of laughter itself becomes a body exercise and is based on the science that the brain (and body) cannot differentiate between real and fake laughter. The results are the same and the individual will receive the same physiological and psychological benefits from the act of laughing whether in response to something funny or contrived; laughing simply for the sake of laughing. Search the term *Laughter Yoga* to learn more about the history and background of Dr. Katari's work in promoting laughter. Since its start there have been more than 60,000 laughter *clubs* established in 60+ countries around the world. There may be a club located near you if you care to check one out in person. The following statement is a short excerpt from the website at **www.laughteryoga.org.**

> It has been scientifically proven that laughter is both preventive and therapeutic. People practicing Laughter Yoga regularly report amazing improvement in their health as well as a more positive mental attitude and higher energy levels. The first thing participants say is that they don't fall sick very often; the frequency of normal cold and flu reduces or even disappears. There are daily reports of partial or total cure of most stress-related illnesses like hypertension, heart disease, depression, asthma, arthritis, allergies, stiff muscles and more. While this sounds fantastic, it all makes perfect sense, as laughter is nature's best cure for stress. For more information and resources go to **www.laughteryoga.org.**

Laughter Yoga is easy and you can have fun trying some exercises in the privacy of your own home. Try it now. There are several kinds of laughter including a nasal little *he-he-he* (the kind of laugh that is discernible but little more than a snicker). Make a heady nasal sound: *he-he-he, he-he-he, he-he-he.* Okay how about a throaty laugh (the kind you might project if you heard a funny story) *ha-ha-ha*. Try it, with your mouth open a little wider: *ha-ha-ha, ha-ha-ha, ha-ha-ha*. Finally, there is a deep belly laugh *ho-ho-ho* (the kind of hearty laugh that Santa Claus might engage in). Give it a try, feel your belly muscles help with the sound *ho-ho-ho, ho-ho-ho, ho-ho-ho*. Now let's put it all together and add some hand claps after each set of laughs. Each set is three groups of three followed by three claps:

He-he-he, he-he-he, he-he-he, **clap-clap-clap**,

Ha-ha-ha, ha-ha-ha, ha-ha-ha, **clap-clap-clap**,

Ho-ho-ho, ho-ho-ho, ho-ho-ho, **clap-clap-clap**.

Try it again, louder and deeper this time and after the ho-ho-ho part, shout "Hooray" when you are done. Ready, set, go.

He-he-he, he-he-he, he-he-ha, **clap-clap-clap**,

Ha-ha-ha, ha-ha-ha, ha-ha-ha, **clap-clap-clap**,

Ho-ho-ho, ho-ho-ho, ho-ho-ho, **clap-clap-clap**.

Hooray!

Do it one more time.

He-he-he, he-he-he, he-he-he, **clap-clap-clap**,

Ha-ha-ha, ha-ha-ha, ha-ha-ha, **clap-clap-clap**,

Ho-ho-ho, ho-ho-ho, ho-ho-ho, **clap-clap-clap**.

Hooray!

Do you feel the endorphins flowing? Isn't it is easy to feel good? Laugh every day!

I will close this chapter with one of my favorite true stories.

The Start of School

Every organization has its own pecking order, the informal chain of command which often is quite different from what is publicized in the formal administrative hierarchy. School districts are no different than any other large organization and while the "Head Principal" is officially listed at the top of the food chain, he or she is only the "boss" in elementary schools. In junior high schools the real person in charge is the head secretary and in every high school on the face of the earth, the individual in charge is the head custodian.

This story is about a couple of junior high schools in two neighboring suburban school districts located in a large metropolitan area. Because the two districts shared a border, kids on one side of a particular street attended school in one district and the kids living on the other side went to the second district.

As you can imagine, there was a lot of movement within the two communities so it was a common occurrence to have families switch their children from one district to the other and that was exactly what happened this one spring.

23

A family living in one community had decided to build a new home within the boundaries of the other. Following protocol, the parents notified the junior high principal in their current home district that they expected their new house to be completed during the summer so they would be moving before school opened in the fall. That principal, Bill J. telephoned the office of the principal (John H.) in the second district.

The John H. was away from the office that day but Bill explained the reason for his call to the head secretary, Mary. Bill and Mary were old friends and they had this same conversation many times in the past with families moving both ways across the districts. It was a courtesy call or a "heads up" until the families actually moved but it was helpful for planning.

Mary informed the neighboring principal that as soon as the new family registered she would call him to send the records over.

Bill said he would keep the file on his desk until he heard back from her and they exchanged good wishes for each to have an enjoyable summer.

The summer months went by quickly and when the principal returned from vacation before school opened in the fall, he noticed the family folder was still on his desk. This family would have two kids in junior high that upcoming year and Bill knew it was important to follow-up on this right away.

The family's name was spelled S-e-c-h-a-u-e-r and pronounced "sex-hour. Bill called over to the other district immediately and Mary answered the phone, "Good morning, Lincoln Junior High School, Mary speaking. How may I help you?"

The principal knew Mary well enough that he did not have to identify himself beyond his first name so he simply went on to say, "Hey Mary, this is Bill at Hopkins, do you have a Sechauer (Sex hour) over there?"

Without even pausing for a breath, Mary replied, "Hell no, we don't even get a coffee break."

"Humour is mankind's greatest blessing." **Mark Twain**

✫✫✫

CHAPTER 3

Be Healthy

82 Years Young

Morris, an 82 year-old man, went to the doctor to get a physical. A few days later, the doctor saw Morris walking down the street with a gorgeous young woman on his arm.

A couple of days after that, the doctor spoke to Morris and said, "You're really doing great, aren't you?"

Morris replied, "Just doing what you said, Doc: *'Get a hot mamma and be cheerful'.*"

A little shocked, the doctor said, "I didn't say that. What I said was...

You've got a heart murmur; be careful."

If one hundred retirees were asked to identify what they believe is the most important thing to have in retirement, 99.9 percent of them will reply "good health." It is the most frequent response given by both genders across all ages, social demographics, and income levels. Over time everyone comes to realize that without good health, no amount of money, time or possessions matter. Most people usually add that they hadn't realized how important it was to have good health, until they or their spouse began to experience an illness or other problems. When ones health starts failing the quality of life changes dramatically. You will find that when you retire, health and healthy-living are topics in the front and center in your thoughts and in conversations with others.

Being conscientious about good health is not anything new for most Baby Boomers and, by this time in our lives, we usually know our particular limitations as well as what we ought to be doing to stay healthy such as eating a nutritious diet (at least most of the time), exercising regularly, getting adequate sleep, reducing stress, and following our doctor's orders. Nevertheless, the new found interest in being healthy when you retire may be for reasons that are different than before including the following:

- You will need to understand Medicare and health insurance options so you can make intelligent choices for your coverage by age 65 and if you are not familiar with insurance, it may require quite a lot of study.

- You may experience a few aches and pains that you didn't notice before and because you are more conscious of your health now. You wish you had listened to your doctor and quit smoking or lost the extra 40 pounds or started walking or done something about stress sooner and scramble to figure out how to address the issues now.

- You watch family, friends and others your age battling diseases and dying.

- You begin to take notice of the many people around you who are dealing with health issues as they talk more about the medicines they take and they drag oxygen tanks and walkers along with them wherever they go.

- Baby Boomers are living longer than ever which results in the possibility of some people being able to stretch their retirements out to 20-25 years or more. You think about how you can be one of those people and you know in order for it to happen you must maintain good health.

For all of those reasons and others, retirees think and talk a lot about health and health- related issues. As some retirees come toe-to-toe with their mortality they seek out ways to stay young and vibrant (and wrinkle free) as they age. Many are searching for the *Fountain of Youth* and a few find it, at least temporarily, at the end of a Botox needle or a liposuction tube or in a pill or a cream. However, common sense tells us that being healthy involves much more than how young we look. It may interest you to know that quite a body of research has been assembled about various populations of people who live the longest in the world today. Researchers leading this work have made some remarkable discoveries about longevity and perhaps they have actually found the elusive *Fountain of Youth*. This chapter is called *Be Healthy* and will primarily focus on some of the more recent research in the area of longevity, a quick look at exercising your mind and a few resources on making healthy lifestyle changes. Chapter 4 is also health-related and is focused on Medicare. It is a separate chapter so that if you have already waded through the river of information and are enrolled in Medicare you can skip the entire discussion if you wish. On the other hand if you have not yet made your Medicare decision, it may be helpful for you to see the summary and a list of official resources available.

Chapter 3 includes the following topics:

- Living to 100 through an introduction to Dan Buettner's book: <u>The Blue Zones, Second Edition: 9 Lessons for Living Longer From the People Who've Lived the Longest</u>.

- A summary of the key results from a survey compiled by *Amelia House* (a senior living provider based in Council Bluffs, Iowa) that examined daily habits of 100 centenarians.

- Excerpts from a Katie Couric interview with ABC Chief Medical Correspondent, Dr. Besser, on the importance of exercising our brains as we age.

- And a few thoughts on longevity, dental check-ups, exercise and more than a few funny jokes.

Chapter 4 will includes the following topic:

- A summary of Medicare and its options (which is a huge topic by itself) including a few hints to help you maneuver through the mountain of legitimate (and bogus) literature you will receive as you approach your 65th birthday.

A LADY'S YEARLY EXAM

I went to the doctor for my yearly physical. The nurse started with certain basics. "How much do you weigh?" she asked.

"135," I said.

The nurse put me on the scale. It turns out my weight is 180.

The nurse asked, "Your height?"

"5 foot 4," I said.

The nurse checked and saw that I only measure 5′ 2″

She then took my blood pressure and told me that it is very high.

"Of course it's high!" I screamed. "When I came in here I was Tall and Slender! Now I'm short and fat.

She put me on Prozac. What a Bitch!

"When your friends begin to flatter you on how young you look, it's a sure sign you're getting old." **Mark Twain**.

✫✫✫

What We Can Learn From the
Blue Zones Research

Some of the most fascinating work in the area of longevity has been done in recent years by Minnesotan Dan Buettner, a National Geographic Fellow. Buettner led a team of demographic and medical researchers around the world in search of what they termed the *Blue Zones*, which are the places where an extraordinarily high proportion of a native population live past 90 years old. *Blue Zones* were so named because of the blue ink that Buettner and his team of researchers used to outline particular areas on world maps developed over more than a decade of study.

In the second edition of his book Buettner writes about a newly identified *Blue Zone* on a Greek island called Ikaria. The research (funded by AARP and National Geographic) showed that one in three Ikarians reaches 90 years old, unlike U.S. Census Bureau statistics which indicate that only one in nine Baby Boomers can expect to live to 90 years old. Buettner and his team made two expeditions to Ikaria. The first one to confirm the longevity of the population by studying birth and death records and a second to determine why people lived so long on this mountainous, windswept and harbor-less island. They discovered several interesting medical phenomena including that Ikarians as a whole suffer significantly less cancer, heart disease, diabetes, depression and dementia than their counterparts in the United States. It is also interesting to note, that in Ikaria the men outlive the women which is also the opposite of life expectancy trends in the United States.

While healthier living and medical advances have pushed life expectancy upward in the United States to 79 (81 for women, 76 for men), we all know some people who live longer. Why is that? Most people agree that a strong gene pool is important for a long and healthy life but Buettner's research indicates that anyone may be able to add on an extra decade or more to their life without taking supplements or requiring extraordinary kinds of exercise. His book, <u>The Blue Zones, Second Edition: 9 Lessons for Living Longer From the People Who've Lived the Longest</u>, is exciting to read and very thought provoking. You may wish to obtain a copy for yourself if you are interested in learning more about this important research.

One of the valuable findings from this report includes identifying the typical diet for the people studied and, like many other healthy long-living populations, Ikarian's eat a healthy Mediterranean-type diet consisting of fruits, vegetables, whole grains, beans, nuts, healthy fats and fish and seafood. The book also presents nine key habits and values (lessons) practiced by the Ikaria centenarian inhabitants. It is important to note that Buettner and his team of researchers identified similar habits being practiced by the inhabitants in four other *Blue Zones* around the world: Sardinia, Italy; Nicoya Peninsula, Costa Rica; Loma Linda, Calif.; and Okinawa, Japan.

The nine lessons learned from the Ikaria study include the following:

1. **Move naturally.** You do not have to run marathons or fanatically exercise, jog or pump iron. Simply do your normal work around the house and garden, walk, cycle, swim, whatever you like to do. Add movement whenever possible like walking around while you talk on the telephone.

2. **Know your purpose.** Have a reason for getting up each morning and have a plan for your time whether it is getting something done for yourself or others.

3. **Kick back.** Find ways to shed stress, whether it's praying, napping, meditating, doing Yoga or going to "Happy Hour."

33

4. **Eat less.** Slow down; let your brain catch up with the amount of food you have eaten and stop eating when you are 80% full.

5. **Eat less meat.** Beans are a key foundation food of most centenarians' diets.

6. **Drink in moderation.** One to two drinks a day.

7. **Have faith.** Denomination was not as important as regularly attending faith-based services.

8. **Love has power.** Always put family first.

9. **Stay social.** Build a social network to support healthy behaviors.

✯✯✯

Living to 100 and the Amelia House Study

Another interesting report on longevity was done by Amelia House, a senior living provider based in Council Bluffs, Iowa, using statistics from the latest U.S. Census and United Health Group's *EverCare 100@100 Survey* . This data provides some insight into the age old "is it nature or nurture" debate. The study indicates that about 20% of one's longevity is tied to genetics and the remaining 80% is based on individual "lifestyle" choices. From the records studied, the Amelia House group compiled a list of "tips" for living to 100 years old and beyond. It is interesting to note the similarities between the results of this study and the information published by Dan Buettner and his team of researchers in the *Blue Zone* research. According to the Amelia House study, five tips to follow to live to 100 or beyond that are practiced by most Americans over the age of 100 are:

- **Socialize** every day

- **Eat** a daily diet full of nutritionally **balanced meals**

- **Sleep** at least **eight hours** every night

- **Laugh** a lot every day (you will appreciate the gray boxes in this book much more now)

- **Be at peace by** praying or meditating every day

Other, less frequently identified traits that seem to be important to fairly high percentages of surveyed seniors that you may also wish to consider are as follows:

- **Volunteer** on a regular basis.

- **Make like a kid** and use modern technology; listen to music on an iPod or similar device, watch

35

YouTube, and send text messages to friends and family members.

Finally, the Amelia House study also reveals that centenarians tend to live in close-knit communities, and many enjoy living "near to nature" where they can walk, visit with friends or family and engage in light exercise outdoors.

The Physical

A 60-year old man went to a doctor for his annual checkup. The doctor told him, "You're in terrific shape. There is absolutely nothing wrong with you. Why you might live forever; you have the body of a 35-year old man. By the way, how old was your father when he died?"

The 60-year old responded, "Did I say he was dead?"

The doctor was surprised and asked, "How old is your father and is he very active?"

The 60-year old replied, "Well he is 82 years old and he still goes skiing three times a season and surfing four times a week during the summer."

The doctor couldn't believe it. So, he asked, "Well how old was your grandfather when he died?"

The 60-year old responded again, "Did I say he was dead?"

The doctor was astonished. He said, "You mean to tell me you are 60 years old and both your father and grandfather are alive? Is your grandfather very active?"

The 60-year old said, "He goes skiing at least once a season and surfing twice a week during the summer. Not only that," said the patient, "my grandfather is 106 years old, and next week he is getting married again."

The doctor said, "At 106-years, why on earth would your grandfather want to get married?"

His patient looked up at the doctor and said, "Did I say he wanted to?"

Two Buddies

A senior citizen said to his eighty-year old buddy:

"So I hear you're getting married?"

"Yep!"

"Do I know her?"

"Nope!"

"This woman, is she real good looking?"

"Not really."

"Is she a good cook?"

"Naw, she can't cook too well."

"Does she have lots of money?"

"Nope! She is poor as a church mouse."

"Well, then, is she good in bed?"

"I don't know."

"Why in the world do you want to marry her then?"

"Because she can still drive!"

✵✵✵

Threats to Longevity

It is worth noting that year after year most medical reports in newspapers, magazines and television shows continue to identify cardiovascular (heart) disease as the number one threat to longevity for Americans. These same sources claim heart disease is responsible for approximately 20% of all disease-related deaths in the United States each year. The three most common traditional risk factors usually identified for heart disease are: high blood pressure, high cholesterol levels, and diabetes. Obviously genetics plays a role as well as other indicators that are indirectly related to heart disease such as obesity. Obesity is linked to high cholesterol levels and diabetes and is also strongly linked to high blood pressure. Therefore as the rate of obesity continues to grow at epidemic proportions so does the prevalence of heart disease risk factors.

Some good news about this topic, however, it is that hypertension, diabetes, high cholesterol levels, and obesity are very often the result of lifestyle choices. This means that each of us can take action and do something about our personal choices to positively impact our health and well-being for many years to come. Lifestyle changes usually involve modifying diet, engaging in consistent rigorous exercise and getting sufficient sleep. You know yourself and you know your specific health issues better than anyone else. I am not a health professional, I do not pretend to be a health professional and even if I were a health professional, you probably would not need me to tell you what to do to get or to stay healthy. In most cases you already know the issues and what you *should* be doing with regard to lifestyle choices. The question may be whether you are following your doctor's orders or just doing your own thing (a few of us have been known to do that a time or two in our lives). Perhaps now is a good time to think about the state of your health and determine if you need to take action like finding the right diet or exercise program and mustering up the resolve to stick with a plan for the sake of your future health and longevity.

On the other hand, perhaps you haven't been to a doctor since the day you were born or when you broke your arm in the 4th grade or when you joined the U.S. Navy in 1968 and you have made it to the age of retirement being completely clueless about your health. If you are one of those rare individuals and really don't know what to do to stay healthy; the place to start would be to consult with your physician or other health care professional who will probably recommend a complete physical examination. Yeah, yeah, we hear you: "If I go for a physical, my doctor might recommend a colonoscopy." That statement is generally followed by the "fear of a colonoscopy" speech that goes something like this: "I am not afraid of a tube that is 2 inches in diameter and 1398.6 foot long going up my petuttie and sliding through every wrinkle and square inch of my colon; seriously I am fine with all that I just don't want to drink all that chalky liquid stuff. I have heard it makes you very uncomfortable."

Yeah, rrriiiigghhtttt, well guess what, the tube isn't 2 inches in diameter or 1398.6 feet long (well, it could be how the hell would I know I am pretty sure I already mentioned I am not a health professional) but I have had two colonoscopies (and slept in a Holiday Inn once) and it wasn't bad either time. Frankly, I do not have any sympathy for you on this one at all, colonoscopies save lives and about that fear of the chalky stuff. Give me a break, the stuff you drink in preparation of a colonoscopy hasn't been chalky for years and, no, it won't taste as good as your evening cocktail and, yes, you will run to the bathroom a few times, but most of the people you know have had one or two or three colonoscopy examinations and trust me, it went just fine. So quit complaining, put your big kid underpants on and just go and do what your physician tells you to do including a colonoscopy if that is part of his/her recommendation! But I digress, and really just intended to encourage you to go to your physician for a thorough baseline physical examination as a place to start your journey to good healthy now and in the future.

To learn more about heart disease or any other medical condition please consult your physician or health care professional. This section and/or book are not intended to be a substitute for the medical advice of physicians. The reader should consult a physician regularly in all matters relating to his/her health and particularly with respect to any symptoms that may require diagnosis or medical attention. If you need a group hug, or other incentives to do that; figure it out you're the adult now and in charge of your own health.

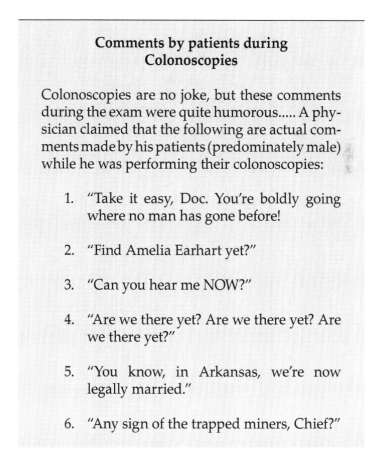

Comments by patients during Colonoscopies

Colonoscopies are no joke, but these comments during the exam were quite humorous..... A physician claimed that the following are actual comments made by his patients (predominately male) while he was performing their colonoscopies:

1. "Take it easy, Doc. You're boldly going where no man has gone before!

2. "Find Amelia Earhart yet?"

3. "Can you hear me NOW?"

4. "Are we there yet? Are we there yet? Are we there yet?"

5. "You know, in Arkansas, we're now legally married."

6. "Any sign of the trapped miners, Chief?"

7. "You put your left hand in; you take your left hand out..."

8. "Hey! Now I know how a Muppet feels! "

9. "If your hand doesn't fit, you must quit!

10. "Hey Doc, let me know if you find my dignity."

11. "You used to be an executive at Enron, didn't you?"

And the best one of all...

12. "Could you write a note for my wife saying that my head is not up here?"

Five Surgeons

Five surgeons from big cities are discussing who makes the best patients to operate on.

The first surgeon, from New York, says, "I like to see accountants on my operating table, because when you open them up, everything inside is numbered."

The second, from Chicago, responds, "Yeah, but you should try electricians! Everything inside them is color coded."

The third surgeon, from Dallas, says, "No, I really think librarians are the best, everything inside them is in alphabetical order."

The fourth surgeon, from Los Angeles chimes in: "You know I like construction workers...those guys always understand when you have a few parts left over."

But the fifth surgeon, from Washington-DC, shut them all up when he observed: "You're all wrong; politicians are the easiest to operate in. There are no guts; no heart, no balls, no brains and no spine, and the head and the ass are completely interchangeable."

Confessions of Emergency Room Doctors

1. A man came into the ER yelling, "My wife's gonna have her baby in the cab!" I grabbed my stuff, rushed out to the cab, lifted the lady's dress, and began to take off her underwear. Suddenly I noticed that there were several cabs --- and I was in the wrong one.

2. At the beginning of my shift I placed a stethoscope on an elderly and slightly deaf female patient's anterior chest wall. "Big Breaths," I instructed. "Yes, they used to be," replied the patient.

3. One day I had to be the bearer of bad news when I told a wife that her husband had died of a massive myocardial infarct. Not more than 5 minutes later, I heard her reporting to the rest of the family that he had died of a "massive internal fart."

4. While acquainting myself with a new elderly patient, I asked, "How long have you been bedridden?" After a look of complete confusion, she answered. "Why, not for about 20 years - when my husband was alive."

5. I was performing rounds at the hospital one morning and while checking up on a woman I asked, "So how is your breakfast this morning?"

"It's very good, except for the Kentucky Jelly. I can't seem to get used to the taste" the patient replied. I then asked to see the jelly and the woman produced a foil packet labeled "KY Jelly."

6. A nurse was on duty in the E.R. when a young woman w/ purple hair styled into a punk rocker Mohawk, sporting a variety of tattoos, and wearing strange clothing, entered. It was quickly determined that the patient had acute appendicitis, so she was scheduled for immediate surgery. When she was completely disrobed on the operating table, the staff noticed that her pubic hair had been dyed green, and above it there was a tattoo that read, "Keep off the grass."

Once the surgery was completed, the surgeon wrote a short note on the patient's dressing, which said, "Sorry, had to mow the lawn."

7. As a new, young MD doing my residency in OB, I was quite embarrassed when performing female pelvic exams. To cover my embarrassment, I had unconsciously formed a habit of whistling softly. The middle-aged lady upon whom I was performing this exam suddenly burst out laughing, further embarrassing me. I looked up from my work and sheepishly said, "I'm sorry. Was I tickling you?"

She replied, "No doctor, but the song you were whistling was, "I wish I was an Oscar Meyer Wiener."

✵✵✵

Don't Forget to Put Your Money
Where Your Mouth Is

A healthy mouth and teeth are also essential components of a
healthy body and over all well-being. According to the American
Dental Association, dentists can tell a lot about your total health
from looking into your mouth. For example, red or inflamed
gums can be a sign of an immune disorder such as diabetes,
rheumatoid arthritis or other underlying health problems, not
necessarily the result of poor oral hygiene.

However, paying attention to good oral hygiene is
extremely important to seniors because this age group is
prone to more tooth decay and infections of the mouth. Not
brushing and flossing can result in bacteria growth and calci-
fied deposits which make it even more difficult to keep teeth
and gums clean and trap food particles left behind after eating. There is also the issue of bad breath which can also be
the result of poor oral hygiene. We have all been subjected to
people whose breath is akin to a port-a-potty at a county fair
in 100 degree heat, and putting aside all the other possible
health concerns, who wants to be remembered for having foul
breath?

Enough on this topic, just don't forget that a dental exam can
do more than reveal cavities and having regular dental check-
ups along with twice daily brushing and flossing can help you
stay well and looking good with a brilliant smile.

The New Dentist

Have you ever been guilty of looking at others
your own age and thinking "Surely I can't look
that old?"

Here is the tale of one woman who didn't think she looked *that* old....

I was sitting in the waiting room for my first appointment with a new dentist. I noticed his DDS Diploma framed and hanging on the wall. It bore his full name and suddenly I remembered a tall, handsome, dark-haired by with the same name that was in my high school class nearly 40 years ago.

"Could he be the same guy?" I wondered remembering that I had a huge crush on him way back then. Upon seeing him, however, I quickly discarded any such thought. This balding, gray-haired man with a deeply lined face was way too old to have been my classmate.

After he examined my teeth, I asked him if he had attended Morgan Park High School.

"Yes, I did. I'm a Mustang," he gleamed with pride.

"When did you graduate?" I asked.

He answered, "In 1968. Why do you ask?"

"You were in my class!" I exclaimed.

He looked at me very closely for a moment. Then that ugly, old, wrinkled, bald, fat, gray, decrepit son-of-a-bitch asked:

"What did you teach?"

***

Be Active

Staying Active

During her physical examination, a doctor asked a middle-aged woman about her physical activity level. The woman said she spent 3 days a week, every week in the outdoors.

"Well, yesterday afternoon was typical; I took a five hour walk about 7 miles through some pretty rough terrain. I waded along the edge of a lake. I pushed my way through 2 miles of brambles. I got sand in my shoes and my eyes. I barely avoided stepping on a snake. I climbed several rocky hills. I went to the bathroom behind some big trees. I ran away from an irate mother bear and then ran away from one angry bull Elk. The mental stress of it all left me shattered. At the end of it all I drank a scotch and three glasses of wine.

Amazed by the story, the doctor said, "You must be one hell of an outdoor woman!"

"No," the woman replied, "I'm just a really, really BAD golfer."

Exercise is another topic that is critical to good health in retirement and, once again, nothing new. If you are already an advocate of exercise you know the benefits of it first-hand. If you are not a fan of exercise then you may be encouraged by a recent article from the Mayo Clinic website where the staff notes many positive effects of adding physical exercise into your routine. The benefits identified include boosting energy levels, helping control weight, improving mood, improving sex life, and improving sleep. It also indicates that regular exercise may improve some health conditions and diseases and will generally help you to feel better and increase the overall quality of life. Check out the Mayo Clinic web site at **www.mayo-clinic.com/health/exercise/.** This site has many more resources on exercise and a host of other health-related topics. Remember always to check with your doctor before starting a new exercise program, especially if you have any health concerns.

A few additional sites that several retired friends and family members use to track healthy eating and exercise habits are: **Fatsecret.com, MyFitnessPal.com** and **SparkPeople.com.** A new Smartphone app that is quickly becoming my personal favorite uses a GPS to track walking or running and is called **RunKeeper.com.** RunKeeper also keeps track of calories and other activities. And there we go with older people using technology again. It is a good thing.

A WOMAN'S FIRST WEEK AT THE GYM

This is dedicated to everyone who ever attempted to get into a regular workout routine

Dear Diary,
For my birthday this year, I purchased a week of personal training at the local health club. Although I am still in great shape since being a high school football cheerleader 43 years ago, I decided it would be a good idea to go ahead and give it a try.

I called the club and made my reservations with a personal trainer named Christo, who identified himself as a 26-year-old aerobics instructor and model for athletic clothing and swim wear.

Friends seemed pleased with my enthusiasm to get started! The club encouraged me to keep a diary to chart my progress.

MONDAY:
Started my day at 6:00 am. Tough to get out of bed, but found it was well worth it when I arrived at the health club to find Christo waiting for me. He is something of a Greek god-- with blond hair, dancing eyes, and a dazzling white smile. Woo Hoo!!

Christo gave me a tour and showed me the machines. I enjoyed watching the skillful way in which he conducted his aerobics class after my workout today. Very inspiring! Christo was encouraging as I did my sit-ups, although my gut was already aching from holding it in the whole time he was around. This is going to be a FANTASTIC week!!

TUESDAY:
I drank a whole pot of coffee, but I finally made it out the door. Christo made me lie on my back and push a heavy iron bar into the air then he put weights on it! My legs were a little wobbly on the treadmill, but I made the full mile. His rewarding smile made it all worthwhile. I feel GREAT! It's a whole new life for me.

WEDNESDAY:
The only way I can brush my teeth is by laying the toothbrush on the counter and moving my mouth back and forth over it. I believe I have a hernia in both pectorals. Driving was OK as long as I didn't try to steer or stop. I parked on top of a GEO in the club parking lot.

Christo was impatient with me, insisting that my screams bothered other club members. His voice is a little too perky for that early in the morning and when he scolds, he gets this nasally whine that is VERY annoying.

My chest hurt when I got on the treadmill, so Christo put me on the stair monster. Why anyone would invent a machine to simulate an activity rendered obsolete by elevators? Christo told me it would help me get in shape and enjoy life. He said some other crap too.

THURSDAY:
Jerkhead was waiting for me with his vampire-like teeth exposed as his thin, cruel lips were pulled back in a full snarl. I couldn't help being a half an hour late-- it took me that long to tie my shoes.

He took me to work out with dumbbells. When he was not looking, I ran and hid in the restroom. He sent some skinny girl to find me. Then, as punishment, he put me on the rowing machine-- which I sank.

FRIDAY:
I hate that Christo more than any human being has ever hated any other human being in the history of the world. He is a stupid, skinny, anemic, anorexic, little aerobics instructor. If there was a part of my body I could move without unbearable pain, I would beat him with it.

Christo wanted me to work on my triceps. I don't have any triceps! And if you don't want dents in the floor, don't hand me the stupid barbells or anything that weighs more than a sandwich.

The treadmill flung me off and I landed on a health and nutrition teacher. Why couldn't it have been someone softer, like the drama coach or the choir director?

SATURDAY:
Satan left a message on my answering machine in his grating, shrilly voice wondering why I did not show up today. Just hearing his voice made me want to smash the machine with my planner; however, I lacked the strength to even use the TV remote and ended up catching eleven straight hours of the Weather Channel.

SUNDAY:
I'm having the church van pick me up for services today so I can go and thank GOD that this week is over.I will also pray that next year my husband will choose a gift for me that is fun-- like a root canal or a hysterectomy. I still say if God had wanted me to bend over, he would have sprinkled the floor with diamonds!!!

Saturday Morning Golf

A couple of women were playing golf one sunny Saturday morning. The first of the twosome teed off and watched in horror as her ball headed directly toward a foursome of men playing the next hole.

Indeed, the ball hit one of the men, and he immediately clasped his hands together at his crotch, fell to the ground and proceeded to roll around in evident agony.

The woman rushed down to the man and immediately began to apologize. She then explained that she was a physical therapist: "Please allow me to help. I'm a physical therapist and I know I could relieve your pain if you'd just allow me!" she told him earnestly.

"Ummph, oooh, nnooo, I'll be alright...I'll be fine in a few minutes," he replied breathlessly as

he remained in the fetal position still clasping his hands together at his crotch. But she persisted; and he finally allowed her to help him.

She gently took his hands away and laid them to the side, loosened his pants and put her hands inside, beginning to massage him. "How does that feel?" she asked.

"It feels great." he replied. "But my thumb still hurts like hell!"

✵✵✵

The Importance of Exercising our Minds

In a recent ABC News broadcast, Chief Health and Medical Editor, Dr. Richard Besser, met with Katie Couric to share some simple tips on living a long and full life. In this feature, Dr. Besser emphasized that it is no big secret that taking care of our bodies by exercising is an essential part of maintaining our overall health, however, the average individual may not be aware that exercising our minds can be equally as important and he encouraged everyone to "use it or lose it." One suggestion of what we might do to exercise our minds and live longer, is to take on new challenges. Not just little challenges like choosing a more difficult crossword puzzle, but hugely challenging activities like learning to speak a new language, taking dance lessons or learning to play an instrument all of which can promote brain function and increase a sense of satisfaction.

Dr. Besser also encouraged viewers to avoid getting too involved in the digital social media world and invest more time in relationships instead. He said he believes that social connections and engagement in the world around us promotes a healthier lifestyle and added that research has shown that higher levels of social connectedness is directly related to lower blood pressure, stronger immune systems, and decreased stress. All of these factors contribute to the prevention of numerous chronic diseases.

Sleep, however, is the activity that Dr. Besser said benefits your health and longevity the most. When we are sleeping our bodies and minds are healing themselves and regenerating. When we do not sleep or our sleep is restless and sporadic, we are not giving ourselves a chance to rejuvenate which can cause long term health issues. He added that sleep deprivation can lead to memory problems, depression, a weakening of an individual's immune system as well as weight gain.

Finally, Dr. Besser suggested that we all get to know our family history which can be valuable in preventing health issues. People who have a close family member with a chronic disease may have a higher risk of developing that same disease than those without such a family connection. If you are aware of health conditions existing in your gene pool you can be conscious of them and take preventative measures or at the very least, detect and treat early.

In summary Dr. Besser, like many others in the field, believes the key to long term health is in creating healthy behaviors by keeping an active body and mind, prioritizing experiences and relationships and making time for rest.

The Bad Accident

A man woke up in the hospital bandaged from head to foot.

The doctor came in and said, "Ah, I see you've regained consciousness. Now you probably won't remember, but you were in a huge pile-up on the freeway. You're going to be okay, you'll walk again and everything, however, your penis was severed in the accident and we couldn't find it."

The man groaned, but the doctor went on, "You have $9000 in insurance compensation coming and we now have the technology to build a new penis. They work great but they don't come cheap. It's roughly $1000 an inch."

The man perked up.

"So," the doctor continued, "You must decide how many inches of a new penis you want.

But I understand that you have been married for over thirty years and this is something you should discuss with your wife. If you had a five incher before and get a nine incher now she might be a bit put out. If you had a nine incher before and you decide to only invest in a five incher now, she might be disappointed. It's important that she plays a role in helping you make a decision on this."

The man agreed to talk it over with his wife.

The doctor came back the next day, "So, he said, "have you spoken with your wife?"

"Yes I have," said the man.

"And has she helped you make a decision?"

"Yes, she has," the man responded.

"And what is your decision?" asked the doctor

"We're getting granite counter tops."

✷✷✷

CHAPTER 4

The Audit

At the end of the tax year, the IRS office sent an inspector to audit the books of a local hospital. While the IRS agent was checking the books, he turned to the CFO of the hospital and said: "I notice you buy a lot of bandages. What do you do with the end of the roll when there's too little left to be of any use?"

"Good question," noted the CFO. "We save them up and send them back to the bandage company and every once in a while, they send us a free roll."

"Oh," replied the auditor, somewhat disappointed that his unusual question had a practical answer. But on he went, in his obnoxious way."What about all these plaster purchases? What do you do with what's left over after setting a cast on a patient?"

"Ah, yes," replied the CFO, realizing that the inspector was trying to trap him with an unanswerable question. "We save it and send it back to the manufacturer and every so often they will send us a free bag of plaster."

"I see," replied the auditor, thinking hard about how he could fluster the know-it-all CFO. "Well," he went on, "What do you do with all the remains from the circumcision surgeries?"

"Here, too, we do not waste," answered the CFO. "What we do is save all the little foreskins and send them to the IRS office, and about once a year, they send us a complete prick."

A Ticket

A Florida senior citizen drove his brand new red Corvette convertible out of the dealership. Taking off down the road, he floored it to 80 mph, enjoying the wind blowing through what little hair he had left. "Amazing!" he thought as he flew down I-75.

Looking in his rearview mirror, he saw the highway patrol behind him, blue lights flashing and siren blaring. "I can get away from him, no problem!" thought the elderly man as he floored it to 100 mph, then 110, then 120. Suddenly, he thought, "What on earth am I doing? I'm too old for this nonsense."

He pulled over to the side of the road and waited for the trooper to catch up with him. Pulling in behind him, the trooper walked up to the driver's side of the Corvette, looked at his watch and said, "Sir, my shift ends in 30 minutes. Today is Friday. If you can give me a reason why you were speeding that I've never heard before, I'll let you go."

The man, looking very seriously at the trooper, said, "Years ago, my wife ran off with a Florida state trooper. I thought you were bringing her back."

"Have a good day, sir," said the trooper.

The Basics of Medicare

Medicare is federally funded health insurance for people 65 years or older, under 65 with certain disabilities, and at any age with End-Stage Renal Disease (ESRD) which is permanent kidney failure requiring dialysis or kidney transplant. When you turn 65 years old, you can enroll in Medicare (often called Original Medicare) Parts A and B.

Disclaimer: The information that follows will provide basic information about the Medicare program provided in good faith and summarized from literature distributed by the U.S. Department of Health and Human Services and the Social Security Administration. It is in no way intended to replace or evaluate information from Medicare, the Social Security Administration or the U.S. Department of Health and Human Services. Nor is the information provided to be construed as advice for any individual.

It will include a list of reliable and official resources for the Medicare program and to request literature and/or information and to ask questions. The most current telephone numbers, web site addresses and postal addresses at the time of this writing are also provided.

Laws and rules governing the Medicare program change from time to time and while all efforts have been made to report accurate and timely information, nothing can replace the *Medicare & You* handbook provided free of cost from the Department of Health and Human Services and the Social Security Administration

Finally, note that this section does not intend to endorse any insurance plan or product, all of which vary by state and area.

Medicare has several parts:

- **Part A** (Hospital Insurance),

- **Part B** (Medical Insurance which includes Medicare covered preventive services---the most familiar are doctor services, clinic calls, and durable medical equipment),

- **Part C** (Advantage Plans which are health plan options that combine Part A, Part B and often Part D coverage),

- **Part D** (Prescription Drug coverage) It is important to note that Medicare monitors the companies selling Part D coverage and you can purchase a standalone prescription drug plan if you do not choose a Medicare Advantage Plan that includes drug coverage.

Original Medicare (Parts A and B) help cover some health-care costs but do not cover all expenses and do not cover prescription drugs. As a result many people enroll in a Medicare health plan to get additional coverage for some of the benefits and services not covered by Medicare and for prescription drug coverage. Medicare covers 80% of <u>Medicare approved</u> procedures. Medigap is a kind of private health insurance that helps pay for some of the health care costs (the "gaps") that traditional or original Medicare doesn't cover, such as deductibles and co-payments. So in the statement above where Medicare covers 80%, a Medigap policy usually covers the other 20% generally you would not have any co-pays for a <u>Medicare approved</u> procedure. If it is a procedure that is <u>not approved</u> by Medicare, <u>you pay all of the cost out of pocket</u>.

Medicare Advantage Plans (which are sold by Medicare-approved private insurance companies) are also required to cover Medicare services, but they do not just fill in the gaps. They provide the usual Medicare-approved services within their own network of doctors and hospitals. To attract clients, most Advantage plans offer some additional services like dental and vision benefits. Advantage plans substitute for traditional or Original Medicare, so you do not (actually cannot) carry a Medigap policy if you join an Advantage plan.

Some people say that individuals who are generally in good health love the Medicare Advantage Plans, but people who need medical care regularly may find that Medicare Advantage Plans can be inexpensive up front but can end up being very expensive overall. If an individual requires hospitalization, co-pays can be very high and the same is true if an individual requires daily medication (prescriptions). Individuals should be prepared for costly co-pays if there is a high probability that they will be hospitalized. It is very important to compare pros and cons of each plan and each kind of plan (Medigap and

Advantage). The plans are listed in the back of the *Medicare &
You* handbook and so that you will be able to see and compare
the out of pocket limits, coverage, etc. and choose the kind of
plan best suited to you.

This section will take a closer look at the various "Parts" of
Medicare and by and large what each covers, then provide some
general information to help define the additional plans available
(Advantage, Medicare Supplement Insurance and Prescription
Drug coverage) and close with a list of resources available online
or that can be downloaded from the Internet or requested at
little or no cost in hard copy from the Department of Health and
Human Services and the Social Security Administration.

Eligibility and coverage is best described in the Medicare
handbook titled *Medicare & You*. Keep in mind that many
insurance brokers sell both Medigap and Medicare
Advantage Plans and can be very helpful in comparing
programs and prices. You can contact your state insurance
department for a list of licensed brokers in your area or
go to Medicare.gov Web site and click on "Compare Drug
and Health Plans" (for Advantage Plans) and "Compare
Medigap Policies" tab. Each will allow you to display plans
and policies available to you in your zip code and allow you
to see prices, benefits and prices. You can also call Medicare
at 800-MEDICARE (633-4227), and ask that the information
be sent to you.

Part A covers:

- **Hospital stays** which includes a semi-private
  room, meals, general nursing, and other hospital services and supplies. It includes care in
  critical access hospitals and inpatient rehabilitation facilities.

- **Skilled nursing facility** care which includes limited coverage of semi-private room, meals, skilled nursing and rehabilitation services, and other services and supplies, following a hospital stay.

- **Home health care services** which can include part-time or intermittent skilled nursing care, and physical therapy, speech-language pathology, and occupational therapy.

- **Hospice care** which includes drugs for pain relief, and medical and support services from a Medicare-approved hospice.

- **It is important to note** that Medicare does not pay for hospital or medical expenses if you are not lawfully present in the United States.

Part B covers:

- **Medical and other services** including doctor's services, outpatient medical and surgical services and supplies, diagnostic tests, durable medical equipment, and more.

- **Clinical laboratory services** including blood tests, urinalysis, and some screening tests.

- **Home health care services** which can include part-time or intermittent skilled nursing care and physical therapy, speech-language pathology, and occupational therapy.

- **An outpatient hospital service which includes the hospital services and supplies** you get as a hospital outpatient.

- **Preventative services** which may help you live a longer healthier life often do not require you to pay anything out-of-pocket as long as you get the service from a doctor (or other qualified health care provider) who accepts_ the Medicare-approved amount as payment in full for covered services.

  This is also known as "accepting assignment." How often and which kinds of services you can receive varies and some services may only be covered for certain people with specific risk factors. The best course of action is to check with your doctor about the specific screenings and services that are right for you.

Part C (Medicare Advantage Plans)

Medicare Advantage Plans are like HMOs or PPOs and are a way to get your Medicare coverage through private companies that are approved by Medicare. These plans are comprehensive and include Part A and Part B and sometimes additional coverage like prescription drugs (Part D). There is usually a monthly premium (in addition to your part B premium) and often a copayment or coinsurance portion that you are responsible for <u>in covered services you receive</u>. Costs, co-pays, additional coverage and rules all vary by plan and company. Individuals, who decide not to join a Medicare Advantage Plan, <u>usually will get Medicare coverage through what is referred to as Original Medicare</u>. If an individual only uses Original Medicare, they can expect to pay 20% out of pocket for Medicare-approved services. (A Medigap policy would pay that 20% for policyholders. The premium would be considerably higher than the Medicare Advantage Plan however there are no co pays.)

Part D (Medicare Prescription Drug Coverage)

Generally speaking Medicare offers prescription drug coverage (Part D) to everyone with Medicare. This coverage is offered through private companies that are approved by Medicare. To get drug coverage you have two choices: 1) you can join a Medicare Prescription Drug Plan (this adds prescription drug coverage to Original Medicare and to certain Medicare Advantage

Plans), or 2) you can join a Medicare Advantage Plan that includes drug coverage.

Number one (1) above is referred to as a stand-alone Prescription Drug Plan. The stand alone Prescription Drug Plan has nothing to do with your health plan, so you could have a health Plan through AARP and a drug plan through Blue Cross. It is very important to compare drug plans annually as there are 30+ companies and they generally modify their coverage and premiums every year, knowing that people hate to change. However, it is not uncommon for it to make a difference of $1000 or more annually in out of pocket expenses for people who take a fair amount of medication. It is very important to compare companies and the place to do it is the official Medicare site at **www.Medicare.gov**. It is an excellent resource or you can locate a **State Health Insurance Assistance Program (SHIP)** counselor. SHIP counselors are free of charge. Most people think when their price increases that it is happening for everyone and that all companies are about the same, but that is not the case and there is a lot of competition in the insurance business.

Usually you have to pay a monthly premium for Medicare prescription drug coverage. It is important to note that if you don't join a Medicare prescription drug plan when you are first eligible, and you do not have other coverage (such as coverage from an employer or union), you may have to pay a late enrollment penalty if you choose to join later. See the *Medicare & You* handbook for exact details.

Once you have a fundamental understanding of the basic parts of Medicare and you are nearing age 65, you will have some decisions to make. If you are confused, don't feel alone. It is a common reaction. Take it one question at a time and ask a trusted friend, family member, SHIP counselor, or the Medicare Office for help (or a referral for help) if you need it.

1. **Do you want to keep Medicare Part B?** If you are already receiving Social Security benefits, you will be automatically enrolled in Part B. If you want to keep the Part B coverage, you do not have to do anything. If however, you do **not** wish to keep Part B, then you must let Medicare (Social Security Administration) know before the effective date printed on the front of your Medicare card which you will receive several months prior to your 65th birthday. The card has very clear instructions about how to return the entire card if you do not choose to participate in Medicare Part B as well as specific instructions on how and when to use the card if you choose to participate in Medicare Part B.

- If you keep Part B, monthly premiums will automatically be deducted from your Social Security benefit payment when your coverage starts. If you do not receive Social Security benefits, you will get a bill for your Part B premium every 3 months.

- If you do not keep Part B when you are first eligible, you may have to wait until a General Enrollment Period (January 1 to March 31 each year) to sign up and your coverage will not start until July 1 of that year. You may also have to pay a late enrollment penalty.

- You may be able to delay joining Part B without a penalty if you or your spouse is working, and you are getting health benefits based on that current employment. Contact your benefits coordinator to see exactly how your insurance plan works with Medicare.

- If you do not want Part B: check the box after the statement "I don't want Medical Insurance" on the back of the Medicare card sent to your home address (about 3 months before your 65th birthday), sign on the back of the card, and send back the entire form (including the card) in the envelope enclosed with that mailing before the effective date listed on the front of the Medicare card. Medicare will send you a new card that shows Part A only.

- To keep Plan B, you don't have to do anything. Simply punch out the designated area to remove the card from the document. Then sign on the front of the Medicare card where indicated. You can begin to use it after the designated start date. The Medicare card is made of stock paper so you may wish to go to an office supply store and have your card laminated.

I refused to let the card out of my sight because it contains my full name and Social Security number. I went to three different office/copy places before they would allow me to watch as they laminated it! I wasn't watching the lamination process; I was watching the person doing the laminating. The first two places of business said I could not come behind the counter because of liability issues, but a local UPS center had the machine right in the front so I could stay behind the counter and still keep a close watch on my highly personal data. Life's simple pleasures!

2. **How will you get your Medicare coverage?** If you decide to keep part B, you can choose how to get your health coverage. You can choose between the Original Medicare (run by the federal government) and a Medicare Advantage Plan (run by a private insurance company).

Original Medicare

- Original Medicare will provide Part A and Part B coverage directly.

- You have your choice of doctors and hospitals that are enrolled in Medicare and accepting new Medicare patients.

- You and/or your supplemental insurance are responsible to pay deductibles and coinsurance.

- You will likely pay a monthly premium for Part B.

- If you want prescription drug coverage, you must choose and join a Medicare Prescription Drug Plan, also know as Part D.

- You can buy a Medicare Supplement Insurance (usually called a Medigap Insurance Policy) to fill in gaps in your coverage. You will pay a monthly premium for this insurance. Medigap insurance typically does not include prescription drug coverage.

Medicare Advantage Plan (also called Part C) includes BOTH Parts A and B.

- Medicare Advantage Plans take over your Medicare Parts A and B so the 80%-20% formula no longer applies as it does in Original Medicare or the Medigap Plans. Private insurance companies (approved by Medicare) provide this coverage.

- In most plans you use specific plan doctors, hospitals or other providers, or you pay more of the costs outside the network.

- You may pay a monthly premium (in addition to your Part B premium---taken from your Social Security benefit or billed separately) and a co-payment or a co-insurance for covered services.

- Most Medicare Advantage Plans include prescription drug coverage. If a particular Advantage plan does not have that coverage, subscribers may be able to join a Medicare Prescription Drug Plan separately.

- If you join a Medicare Advantage plan you cannot be sold a Medigap insurance policy, too.

It is important to note that some individuals may be able to join other types of Medicare health plans such as the Medicare Cost Plan or Programs of All-Inclusive Care for the Elderly (PACE) or get services through various pilot programs to help certain groups of seniors. There are some other important differences between Original Medicare and a Medicare Advantage Plan. Medical Advantage Plans available in your area may include Health Maintenance Organizations (HMOs), Preferred Provider Organization Plans (PPOs), Private Fee-for-Service (PFFS) Plans, or Special Needs Plans (SNP). To compare Medicare Advantage Plans available in your area visit: **www.medicare.gov/find-a-plan.**

Some questions that may help you decide between Original Medicare and a Medicare Advantage Plan might include the following:

- Are the services I need covered?

- Is doctor or hospital choice important?

- Do I travel a lot and if so what kind of coverage will I have from one state to the next? Remember that Medicare does not cover you if you travel outside the United States.

- Do I have health insurance from an employer (or a spouse's employer)?

- Is my health generally good and am I willing to take the risk that it will stay that way?

If you select a plan and find you are not as happy with it as you thought you were going to be, there is an opportunity to make changes annually. During the open enrollment period between October 15 and December 7 each year, you can join or switch plans. If you make a change during this time frame, your new coverage will take place starting January 1 of the following year. If you are in a Medicare Advantage Plan, you can leave your plan and switch to Original Medicare from January 1 to February 14. If you make that change you will also have until February 14 to join a Medicare Prescription Drug Plan. You can change a Medigap Plan to another Medigap Plan anytime but another plan can turn you down if you are outside the open enrollment period.

Selecting between Original Medicare and a Medicare Advantage Plan is very personal and different factors apply for each individual. It is very important to review and compare the different plans and coverage of benefits available in your area and be sure you understand the rules and any limitations that apply.

1. **Do you want or need prescription drug coverage (part D)?** If you choose Original Medicare and want drug coverage, you will have to join a Medicare Prescription Drug Plan. If, instead of Original Medicare, you choose to join a Medicare Advantage Plan, you will want to

check with the plan administrator to be sure that it includes Medicare drug coverage. However you will also want to compare those Advantage plans <u>without prescription coverage</u> and add the cost of a standalone Prescription Drug Plan if you choose that coverage.

- Medicare prescription drug plans are run by private companies that contract with Medicare, and as a result there may be dozens of different plans available where you live. All Medicare prescription drug plans offer at least the standard prescription drug coverage, but costs, co-pays and coverage are different with every plan. It is very important to compare Prescription Drug Plans every year between October 15th and through December 7th. It will save you money!

- You may have prescription drug coverage from an employer, union, TRICARE at the Department of Veterans Affairs (VA), the Federal Employees Health Benefits (FEHB) or other programs. If you participate in any mentioned above or others, check with your plan administrator before you make any changes to your current plan.

- Your monthly prescription drug premium may be higher if your modified adjusted gross income is above certain levels and the amounts can change every year depending upon your income.

- If you have limited income you may qualify for Extra Help. See your *Medicare & You* handbook for exact details on where to find out if you qualify. This can be a tremendous savings for those who qualify. You can apply online by going to www.SSA.Gov (official site).

- If you do not join a Medicare prescription drug plan when you are first eligible for Medicare and you go without creditable prescription drug coverage for 63 days or more in a row, you may have to pay a late enrollment penalty to join a plan later. If you qualify for Extra Help paying for prescription drug costs, you can join a Medicare prescription drug plan at any time without a penalty.

2. **Do you want or need a Medicare Supplement Insurance (Medigap) insurance policy?** If you choose Original Medicare, you may want to buy a policy that helps pay some of the costs not covered by Medicare. You do not need and cannot purchase or use a Medigap policy if you choose a Medicare Advantage Plan.

- Medigap policies are a type of private insurance designed to pay some of your out-of-pocket expenses not covered by Medicare. Medigap Policies only cover expenses that are Medicare-approved. Medicare, however, only pays 80%, so you will need the Medigap Policy to pay the other 20% if you want full coverage.

- Some Medigap policies may say they will offer emergency care outside of the United States, which is not covered under Original Medicare. Be sure to check the fine print on your Medigap Policy before you travel internationally. Usually for a service to be covered, it must be a Medicare-approved service otherwise neither Medicare or the Medigap Policy will pay and keep in mind that Medicare will not cover medical expenses outside the United States. You likely will need a separate policy to cover you during travel outside the United States. Check this carefully if it applies to you. Medicare does not pay for hospital or medical expenses if you are not lawfully present in the United States.

- You need both Part A and Part B to buy a Medigap policy.

- Medigap policies are identified by letters in most states and must have standardized benefits which mean you can easily compare a plan "F" sold by one company with a plan "F" sold by another company.

- Medigap policies do not cover long-term care, vision, dental care, private duty nursing care, or prescription drug coverage.

- All policies may not be available in all states.

- Each Medigap policy only covers one person. You and your spouse must purchase separate Medigap policies. Some couples ask if there are benefits or price breaks if they both get the same policy from the same insurance company. The short answer is, "no". There is not a discount or any benefit if both spouses buy from the same company so it does not make any difference. Most states have premium comparisons on their websites listed under their Insurance Commissioner's webpage so each of you can choose a plan tailored to your health needs.

- Costs of Medigap insurance vary depending upon where you live and which company you choose so <u>always compare coverage and cost</u>.

- You will pay a monthly premium directly to the private company in addition to your Part B premium (billed every three months by the Social Security Administration (SSA) or automatically deducted from your SSA benefits each month).

- The best time to buy Medigap insurance is during the 6-month period that starts with the first month you turn 65 years old. This is your open enrollment period and you can buy any Medigap policy sold in your state without any questions asked. After this enrollment period you may have to pay higher premiums or may not be able to get the policy you want. Be sure to compare premiums online at your state's Insurance Commissioner's site.

If you are retired and have retiree health insurance coverage through your former employer, Medicare will become your primary health insurance. Medicare will pay its portion of the costs and the amount not covered can be submitted to your employer's plan. However, it is always advisable to check with your benefits administrator to find out how Medicare Parts A and B work with your current company plan.

The same is true if you are still working and carry your spouse on your employee health plan and your spouse is approaching age 65. There are many different options depending upon whether one or both individuals are retired or not and if either is receiving Social Security benefits. It is complicated so if you are enrolled in a employer healthcare plan, meet in person to go over your coverage and options, ask questions, take notes, get everything in writing, date your report and keep it in your files. This may not be a one-time meeting because plans and benefits may change over time as does Medicare and its options, so it is advisable to review insurance changes annually and meet with your employer benefits coordinator or whenever you have any questions.

Also some people may be able to get help from their state to pay for some Medicare premiums. In some cases Medicare savings programs may be available to help qualifying individuals pay for Medicare Part A and B, deductibles, and copayments if certain requirements are met. These programs are: Qualified Medicare Beneficiary Program (QMB), Specified Low-Income Medicare Beneficiary Program (SLMB), and the Qualified Individual Program (QI) and the Qualified Disabled and Working Individuals Program (QDWI).

QMB is the most comprehensive and may provide qualifying individuals with coverage for Medicare Part A and Part B premiums, along with deductibles for Medicare covered services. Individuals who are entitled to Medicare Parts A and B and whose income is no more than 100 percent of the federal poverty limit may qualify for QMB.

SLMB pays only for Medicare Part B premiums and may be available to individuals who receive Medicare Part A and whose income is between 100 percent and 120 percent of the poverty limit.

QI is an extension of SLMB and also pays for Medicare Part B premiums to a limited number of individuals whose income is between 120 percent and 135 percent of the poverty level. The QDWI helps pay for Part A premiums if you are a working disabled person under age 65 and are not receiving medical assistance from your state. Call your state Medicaid Program for more information and to check eligibility for any of these programs or go to **www.medicare.gov/your-medicare-costs/ help-paying-costs/**.

The most reliable information and resources come directly from Medicare and the Social Security Administration (**ALWAYS CHOOSE THE OFFICIAL SITE**). Below is a list including a brief description of some of the kinds of information each agency offers.

- **Medicare Helpline – 1-800-633-4227 (TTY users call 1-877-486-2048)**

  www.Medicare.gov

- Get answers to all of your Medicare questions 24 hours a day, 7 days a week. Also a list of Medicare health and prescription drug plans available in your area. Information on Medicare Savings Programs, Medicaid, Supplemental Security Income (SSI), and Extra Help with prescription drug costs.

- **Social Security Administration Office - 1-800-772-1213 (TTY users call 1-800-325-0778)**

  www.socialsecurity.gov

Get answers to your questions about Social Security retirement or disability benefits and get extra help paying for all or part of your Medicare plan. Social Security personnel are available from 7am to 7pm Monday - Friday.

Get information about enrolling in Medicare or correcting your Medicare card, help paying for Medicare prescription drug coverage or changing your address.

- **State Health Insurance Assistance Program (SHIP)**
  For your local SHIP phone number, visit **www.medicare. gov/contacts** or call **1-800-MEDICARE**

Free personalized health insurance counseling and help making health coverage decisions.

- **Medicare Coordination of benefits Contractor (COBC)**
  1-800-999-1118
  (TTY 1-800-318-8782)

Find out if Medicare or your other insurance pays first. Let Medicare know that you have other insurance, or if you need to report changes about your insurance information.

- **Department of Health and Human Services, Office for Civil Rights**

  1-800-368-1019   **(TTY: 1-800-537-7697)**

  www.hhs.gov/ocr

Check on your rights if you believe you have been discriminated against because of your race, color, religion, national origin, disability, age or sex.

- **Federal Trade Commission**
  1-800-MEDICARE ID Theft Hotline at 1-877-438-4338

  TTY: 1-866-653-4261

  Protect yourself from Medicare fraud and ID theft.

- **Department of Defense – 1-866-773-0404 TTY 1-866-773-0405 1-877-363-1303 (Pharmacy) TTY Pharmacy 1-877-540-6261**

  Get information about TRICARE for Life and TRICARE Pharmacy Program.

  www.tricare.mil/mybenefit

- **Department of Veterans Affairs – 1-800-827-1000 TTY 1-800-829-4833**

  For information if you are a veteran or have served in the U. S. military.

  www.va.gov

- **Office of Personnel Management – 1888-767-6738 (1-800-878-5707**

  For information about the Federal Employee Health Benefits Program for current or retired federal workers.

  www.opm.gov/insure

- **Railroad Retirement Board (RRB) – 1-877-772-5772 TTY 1-312-751-4701**

  www.rrb.gov

- **Quality improvement Organization (QIO)
  1-800-MEDICARE**

  To ask questions or file complaints about the quality of care for Medicare-covered services.

Will I live to see 80?

I recently picked a new primary care doctor. After two visits and exhaustive lab tests, she said I was doing fairly well for my age. (I am past Sixty Five).

A little concerned about that comment, I couldn't resist asking her, "Do you think I'll live to be 80?"

She asked, "Do you smoke tobacco, or drink beer, wine or hard liquor?"

"Oh no," I replied. "I'm not doing drugs, either!"

Then she asked, "Do you eat rib-eye steaks and barbecued ribs?"

"I said, 'Not much... My former doctor said that all red meat is very unhealthy!"

"Do you spend a lot of time in the sun, like playing golf, boating, sailing, hiking, or bicycling?"

"No, I don't," I said.

She asked, "Do you gamble, drive fast cars, or have a lot of sex?"

"No," I said...

She looked at me and said, "Then, why do you even give a shit how long you live?"

✶✶✶

What to do with all the Junk Mail?

If you are within a year of your 65th birthday and have not already started receiving junk mail regarding Medicare choices; trust me, you will. Many, many, many postcards and letters will arrive nearly every day and by the dozens some weeks. There will be full sized letters on stationery, tri- fold cards with return postage paid and others on card stock that include a pre-addressed return envelopes. Each one appears to be quite *official* and most request personal information such as your birth date, social security number, spouse's name and birth date, verification of your address and so forth. Each one is to be returned to an important sounding office at a "Processing Center" some-where---in fact there must be "Processing Centers" on every corner, in every city and town, everywhere!! Clearly they are all P.O. boxes in cities across the country. Some are stamped *URGENT* or state in bold print that you will lose benefits in a period of time (usually 10-15 days) if the information is not returned. Some will be in oversized brown (official looking) envelopes with official looking seals trying to appear as though they came from an actual government agency. It is an attempt to be similar to the legitimate correspondence you will receive from the Social Security Administration so be careful to deter-mine if it is genuine or not. Others will be printed on bright yellow or pink card stock paper to signal a sense of urgency. If you are unsure whether it is actual correspondence from the Social Security Administration (SSA), you can call the SSA office and describe it or you can check with a local State Health Insurance Assistance Program (SHIP) counselor.

A pink colored official looking card arrived in my mail today. Bold lettering proclaimed that is was *the* official source for changes in Medicare for this year and in order for me to receive that essential information (to be able to make my Medicare deci-sions) I was asked to provide certain personal information and verify my identity. Only after confirming my identity would they provide that critical information to me. At the bottom of the card was a message reminding me that if this card was not returned within 15 days I would not be eligible to take advantage of current year Medicare changes. It was nothing more than a piece of trash used to obtain personal information. It is absolutely amazing to see the methods some people and companies use to mislead consumers. Nevertheless, deception is happening all the time and will continue to happen to seniors. It is very confusing to know what is real, what is not and what to do about it? Do you respond to it, discard it or destroy it? What if it really did come from the SSA? How does one know?

Any "official" information from the U.S. Government is going to come from the Social Security Administration, Medicare, or the Department of Health and Human Services (addresses are listed at the end of the Medicare section in this chapter); never from a *Processing Center* and never returned to a P.O. Box. Look at the return address and if it isn't from one of those three departments with an actual street address, then my personal suggestion is to do the following: 1) go to the department store of your choice, 2) purchase a good quality cross-cutting shredder, and 3) use it often for all of the junk mail items that come to your door from Processing Centers everywhere. You will find countless other good uses for a shredder because many unscrupulous companies and many unscrupulous people believe retirees are looking for ways to spend their money and they send a lot of offers through the mail that contain preapproved offers with your name and address printed on them. They should all be shredded, too. I would like to complain about it more, but frankly it may be the only thing keeping the U.S. Postal Service in business so as long as you are vigilant in screening out the fakes, all is good.

Never send the card back and never provide personal information to a processing center. I have discovered that most of these requests for information are insurance companies on a "fishing trips" hoping you will bite. If you wish to have an insurance representative call on you in person to explain a Medicare Advantage Plan, Medigap Policy and/or a Medicare Prescription Drug Plan, then use the resources provided for in your *Medicare & You* Handbook to review the insurance plans available in your state and contact the company or companies of your choice directly. A representative will communicate with you in person very quickly (usually faster than the speed of light) and you can invite them into your home or meet with them at an office and decide if you wish to purchase a product from them. In that case it is perfectly appropriate to share your personal information to make an application for a policy. Otherwise, the best rule is not to share any personal information with strangers on the phone, in correspondence or even if they show up on your doorstep in person. Happy shredding!

Deer Camp

Four guys had been going to the same deer camp for many years.

Two days before the group is to leave,

Ron's wife puts her foot down and told him he isn't going.

Ron's friends are very upset that he can't go, but what can they do.

Two days later the three get to the camping site only to find Ron sitting there with a tent set up, firewood gathered, and dinner cooking on the fire.

"Dang man, how long you been here, and how did you talk your wife into letting you go?"

"Well, I've been here since yesterday. Yesterday evening,

I was sitting in my chair and my wife came up behind me and put her hands over my eyes and said, 'Guess who'?"

"I pulled her hands off my eyes, and saw that she was wearing a brand new black lace nightie.

She took my hand and pulled me to our bedroom. The room had candles lit and rose petals scattered all over the place.

On the bed she had handcuffs, and ropes! She told me to tie and cuff her to the bed, and I did.

And then she said, 'Do whatever you want'.

So....... Here I am."

Who's a Turkey?

A DNR officer was driving down the road when he came upon a young boy carrying a wild turkey under his arm.

He stopped and asked the boy, 'Where did you get that turkey?'

The boy replied, 'What turkey?'

The game warden said, 'That turkey you're carrying under your arm.'

The boy looks down and said, 'Well, lookee here, a turkey done roosted under my arm!'

The game warden said, 'Now look, you know turkey season is closed, so whatever you do to that turkey, I'm going to do to you.

If you break his leg, I'm gonna break your leg. If you break his wing, I'll break your arm. Whatever you do to him, I'll do to you. So, what are you gonna do with him?'

The little boy said, 'I guess I'll just kiss his ass and let him go!'

✮✮✮

CHAPTER 5

Simplify Your Life

Story of a Robot

A father bought a lie detector robot that would slap people when they lied. He decided to test it out at dinner that night so the father asked his son what he did that day.

The son said, "I did some schoolwork." The robot slapped the son.

The son then said, "Ok, Ok. I was at a friend's house watching a movie."

Dad asked, "What movie did you watch?"

Son said, "Toy Story." Once again, the robot slapped the son.

The son quickly fessed up, "Ok, Ok we were watching porn."

Dad said, "What? At your age I didn't even know what porn was!"

The robot slapped the father.

Mom laughed loudly and said, "Well he certainly is *your* son!"

The robot slapped the mother!

End of Story

P.S. Robot for Sale

After years of working, managing deadlines, goals and company agendas then going home to equally demanding to-do lists and over-scheduled calendars, most people on the verge of retirement long to be less busy and to enjoy less complicated and more organized lives. Many people at this age also come to the realization that they have acquired too many possessions over the years and no longer use much of what they have, let alone remember where everything is even located. As a result many boomers are very clear about their desire to simplify their lives and, in addition, are determined to downsize their supersized lifestyles as they prepare for a calmer and more peaceful pace in retirement.

The words "simplify your life," sound uncomplicated enough but can mean something different to each individual and, so everyone has to determine what it is about his/her life that needs to be simplified. The quest for a simple life often begins with de-cluttering, downsizing and organizing ones environment which includes belongings, schedules and commitments. It is a process of finding balance and it is usually different for each

individual. For many it means dealing with unfinished projects or shoe boxes filled with photographs that never made it
into albums or by sorting through piles of memorabilia, clothes,
cleaning out a garage or attic, reducing commitments or something else entirely. While there are many ways to approach the
task of simplifying one's life, it often begins with getting organized through de-cluttering, and downsizing. Over my lifetime
organizing has become as much a second nature as slipping into
a warm sweater on a cold winter day. However, that is not necessarily true for others, particularly those who have lived in the
same house for many years. Having moved several times including once across the country, I have a lot of experience in this area
and am often asked for advice by other retirees who are ready
to scale back their belongings, sell their houses, and move into a
retirement home. Transitioning from working to retired life can
be more challenging and disruptive than expected and the process of de-cluttering, downsizing and organizing can be helpful
in bringing balance within ones grasp.

This chapter will include some of what I have learned
through personal experience and a few tips discovered in articles and online that may also be helpful. If the process seems
overwhelming to you, keep in mind that helping Baby Boomers
transition into retirement is big business today and there are
thousands of companies and non-profit organizations in the
country that are willing to assist clients with every aspect of
moving. You do not have to feel overwhelmed or that you cannot complete the entire task by yourself. For a fee professionals will come into your home and take care of de-cluttering by
removing unwanted items and organizing your belongings
for you. If you prefer to do the work yourself, they will do the
"heavy lifting" to assist you in meeting your goals. Either way
it is usually a win-win and gets you to a simpler more balanced
life sooner!

"Three Rules of Work: Out of clutter find simplicity; From
discord find harmony; In the middle of difficulty lies opportunity." **Albert Einstein**

24 MPH!

Sitting on the side of the road waiting to catch speeding drivers, a Massachusetts state trooper sees a car puttering along at 24 mph. He thinks to himself, "This driver is as dangerous as a speeder!" So he turns on his lights and pulls the driver over.

Approaching the car, he notices that there are five elderly ladies - two in the front seat, and three in the back, wide-eyed and white as ghosts. The driver, obviously confused, says to him, "Officer, I don't understand. I always try to drive the exact speed limit. What seems to be the problem?"

The trooper, trying to contain a chuckle, explains to her that "24" was the Route number, not the speed limit. A bit embarrassed, the woman grinned and thanked the officer for pointing out her error.

"But before you go, Ma'am, I have to ask, is everyone in this car OK? These women seem awfully shaken."

"Oh, they'll be all right in a minute, officer. We just got off Route 105."

✧✧✧

De-Cluttering

It is truly amazing to catch a glimpse into some people's garages as one drives down any street in any town or city in the United States. Many are piled high to the ceilings with boxes, tubs and loose stuff; often filled with so much clutter there is not even room for the owner's vehicle which is, of course, the primary purpose for the garage in the first place. Retirement is a great time to do an inventory of your belongings and to think about your possessions as you consider your personal affairs.

Paring down a lifetimes' worth of possessions is no easy task, but at the end of the day your peace of mind and sense of accomplishment in knowing what you have and where it is located is worth the trouble of sorting through it all. In addition the importance of cleaning, de-cluttering and organizing cannot be over-stated especially if you are considering selling your house. An unintended but positive consequence of de-cluttering can also be the feeling of enjoyment you will experience when you donate things you no longer use to others who can use them. It is not only personally gratifying but also good for the world we live in.

First choose an area or room where you will start, then take a moment to mentally prepare yourself for the task ahead by picturing what you hope to accomplish when you are finished with the particular area (begin with the end in mind). Ask yourself a few questions: What do you want it to look like when it is finished? What are your goals for this room or area (how do you plan to use it in the future)? Do you intend to un-stack all of the stuff stored in that designated space, clean it and just put it back where you found it---presumably in neater piles---or are you are ready to lose some of it?

Once you have an idea of what you want to accomplish and you are motivated and willing to take on the entire task yourself, start with one room or one area (such as the garage or attic) or if that seems too overwhelming, start with one room, a closet or even a single cabinet. Set a goal of identifying a space and getting that one space de-cluttered in one day. It will get you started on your de-cluttering journey and help you develop a system and a rhythm. Don't worry about not getting everything done right away, it takes time and may be a slower process in the beginning because you may start out obsessing about each item but as you get into the rhythm of it, the task usually becomes easier and letting go of things usually becomes easier, too. The idea is to start somewhere and get to work. Seeing one area de-cluttered, clean and organized will likely motivate you to continue into the next area.

However, if just thinking about sorting and cleaning causes you to break out in a cold sweat and makes you feel anxious, you may need to take a step back and determine whether this is something you can actually handle on your own or if you need help. If you decide you need help, you may consider asking an adult child, a close friend or a neighbor to pitch in for a few days. Many cities also have volunteer organizations available to assist seniors with projects such as this. Additionally there are companies that offer the services of professional organizers for a fee, so if the task seems daunting and you have the financial means to do it, hiring someone to help you may be another option. Those who hire professional organizers say it is a good investment because the professionals keep them focused on the project and on schedule. There is the added benefit of having an organizational coach throughout the entire process which substantially reduces the stress that is usually involved in this process. Most of the companies that help seniors with sorting and de-cluttering will also organize and carry out a yard or estate sale of unwanted items for you. Often the money brought in from the sale will offset the cost of the services and will save you the stress and anxiety of all of the work.

Let's assume, however, that you are going to give de-cluttering and downsizing a try on your own. First clear a day on your calendar and identify an area where you will start de-cluttering.

Then decide if you are willing to have a sale of unwanted items later or if you will give them to charity, and obtain four large boxes, tubs or bins. Label the boxes, tubs or bins in the following way:

1. Love It

2. Use It

3. Lose It

4. Trash It

As the labels imply, you must decide which of the four boxes each item in the space will go into and to make that determination, EVERY item in that area must be held to the "litmus test" of two simple questions, 1) do you love it or 2) do you use it? If you answer "yes" to **either** of those questions then you keep it, if you answer "no" to both of the questions, it is time to get rid of that item. It can be placed in the *Lose It* box or thrown directly into the *Trash It* pile depending upon the items' condition. Collections, books, old correspondence or magazines are examples of belongings that may have grown out of control. It is time to simplify and let them go.

You may wish to use the following guide to help you determine which box each item is placed, but first before you start, repeat the following statement out loud: The best things in life are not things. The best things in life are not things. The best things in life are not things. The best things in life are not things. Okay, you get the idea and should have a little more resolve and be in the right frame of mind to get started now.

Place the four large boxes or containers in close proximity to the space you have designated to de-cluttered. Breaking the project into smaller parts may be helpful, so if you have selected a spare room for example; to get started you will need to completely empty one area, closet, drawer or cabinet at a time. As you remove each item, identify which box it will go into and continually remind yourself that everything must go into one of them.

Love It Box: If it is something that holds sentimental or financial value and even though you may not use, wear or display it very often, you know in your heart that you truly love it and you must keep it. You may have forgotten about this item because it has been tucked away in a box or closet for so long and you may even consider ways you can enjoy it more in the future, or you may wish to pass it along to someone else to enjoy, but for now you will simply make the decision to keep it because it has emotional meaning for you and place it in the *Love It* box and move on to the next item.

Use It Box: If an item is something you use, notwithstanding the frequency of use, and it is in good working condition place it in the U*se It* box. Frequency of use is not as significant as the fact that you do actually use it. For example the item may be a Lefsa griddle that is pulled out once a year for creating special holiday foods for your family or a cordless drill that is used frequently throughout the year to fix or assemble things. Both items are equally important **if** you use them and **if** they are in good working condition. Remember it is critical that all items placed in the *Use It* box meet both standards in that statement; you must use it and it must be in good working condition. It does not count if you say to yourself that *if* it was in working order you *would* use the item. Face it, if you haven't gotten around to fixing it by now, it ain't gonna happen. If that is the conversation going on in your head, place it in the *Lose It* box.

Lose It Box: If you answered no to both of the questions: 1) *do you love it* or, 2) *do you use it*, then the item goes into one of the two remaining containers, either the *Lose It* box or the *Trash It* box. *Lose It* is fairly self explanatory, but keep in mind that this category includes recycling the items by donating or selling them. You may need several boxes for this category because it usually ends up with the largest amount of items. You can give your unwanted items in the *Lose It* category to a charitable organization or to someone you know as a gift, or you can hold a yard/garage sale later. It is best to set a date for the yard/garage sale and let friends know, print signs etc. because it will be a goal for you to work towards and you won't end up with a clean orderly house attached to the garage described at the beginning of this chapter.

If you know some people who might enjoy the things you are ready to discard, invite them over to your home to peruse the items and select anything they want (for free) before you haul it off to a charitable organization or hold a sale later. In either case you are recycling goods, that still work and are useable or are things of beauty, to someone you care about. It is all good.

If you think some of the items have some value, you may want to try selling them at a yard or garage sale, on eBay, Craigslist or some other local venue. Often, it is easier to schedule a charity pick-up than go through the added work of a sale. There is an added bonus for donating goods, if you keep a list of items along with a fair market value, you can take a charitable donation deduction on your income taxes at the end of the year. On the other hand if you enjoy holding yard sales, go for it. You will likely fill many *Lose It* boxes so be sure to designate a large area (like your garage) to place all of these boxes temporarily. Each item will have to be priced and prepared for sale after you have sorted through your entire household and are ready to hold the sale.

The **Trash It** box is for all items that are no longer working, have parts missing, and are broken, dirty, faded and basically unusable. Just throw them away and save someone else the trouble of doing it after they have expended the manpower and wasted gas to haul it to a charity workshop. If you anticipate having a lot of trash, you can contact a local trash company and they will bring a large receptacle right to your front yard for your convenience. Be sure to check whether they take old appliances and electronics before placing those items in a general trash container.

Once you have completed the de-cluttering process by identifying what you want to keep and have hauled out what is trash, it can be fun to host that "Free Merchandise Party" mentioned earlier. You can display all of the items in the *Lose It* boxes and invite family, friends and neighbors to help themselves to the goods at no charge. This kind of event will allow you to share some of the items that have sentimental value and the memories they represent with others who mean something to you. Make it a celebration, serve snacks, provide bags and boxes (to help people pack their treasures), and take photos of the gathering to remember and create a record of what you gave away. Every step of de-cluttering feels good. Enjoy it!

Be Careful What you Wish For

A man walked into a restaurant with a full-grown ostrich behind him, and as he sat down, the waitress came over and asked for their order. The man said, "I'll have a hamburger, fries and a coke," and turned to the ostrich. "What's yours?"

"I'll have the same," said the ostrich.

A short time later the waitress returned with the order. "That will be $6.40 please," and the man reached into his pocket and pulled out the exact change for payment.

The next day, the man and the ostrich came again and the man said, "I'll have a hamburger, fries and a coke," and the ostrich said, "I'll have the same." Once again the man reached into his pocket and paid with the exact change.

This became a routine until late one evening, the two entered again. "The usual?" asked the waitress.

"No, this is Friday night, so I will have a steak, baked potato and salad," said the man.

"Same for me," said the ostrich.

A short time later the waitress came with the order and said, "That will be $12.62." Once again the man pulled the exact change out of his pocket and placed it on the table.

The waitress couldn't hold back her curiosity any longer and said. "Excuse me, sir. How do you manage to always come up with the exact change out of your pocket every single time?"

"Well," said the man, "several years ago I was cleaning the attic and I found an old lamp. When I rubbed it a Genie appeared and offered me two wishes. My first wish was that if I ever had to pay for anything, I would just put my hand in my pocket, and the right amount of money would always be there."

"That's brilliant!" says the waitress. "Most people would wish for a million dollars or something, but you'll always be as rich as you want for as long as you live!"

"That's right! Whether it's a gallon of milk or a Rolls Royce, the exact money is always there," said the man.

The waitress asked, "One other thing, sir, what's with the ostrich?"

The man sighs, paused, and answered, "My second wish was for a tall chick with long legs who agrees with everything I say!"

✩✩✩

Downsizing

Many of us upsized our homes over our working years to accommodate growing families and an increasing number of possessions, but now as Baby Boomers on the verge of retirement, we see our nests empty and downsizing is becoming increasingly more appealing. For the majority of American families, housing is the largest monthly expenditure and carrying a big house with a big mortgage payment into retirement may not be an option for many retirees. Most retirees have reduced income when they retire, but even so many may actually have more options when it comes to housing because they are not tied down to a particular location anymore and many discover that if it's too difficult to make ends meet while living in their old house, moving may be a better option than getting into financial trouble.

Deciding where to live is one of the first big questions facing retiring Baby Boomers today. Do you want to stay in your family home? Is it financially possible? Many retirees decide it is time to give up the family home for something smaller with less upkeep and fewer responsibilities or a condo or a townhome with no yard duties at all. Others decide to keep the family home and buy a second home or cabin in another area for some time to relax close to nature.

My spouse and I have numerous friends and colleagues who have sold their family homes and purchased or rented other places to live. Everyone has made the changes that meet their needs. One couple rents a small home in a 55+ resort community in Mesa, Arizona for six months and a cabin at a lake in northern Minnesota the remaining six months of the year. They choose to not own at all and find it very "freeing" not to have to deal with appliances that stop working or doors that need adjusting, or gophers digging holes in the yard, etc. They simply call their landlord if a problem arises.

A woman friend (single) sold her home and bought a small Recreation Vehicle (RV). She travels across the country in her RV visiting friends and relatives along the way and essentially vacationing and sightseeing all year long. She travels the southern half of the United States in the fall and winter months and the northern half in the spring and summer.

Other friends sold their home in the suburbs of a metropolitan area and purchased a condo in the heart of the city. They wanted to get away from upkeep of a big yard and house and to be in close proximity to professional sports, opera, and the theater. A few others have gone the opposite direction from the city and purchased small houses in small towns and rural areas so they can get closer to nature and work at vegetable gardening and pursue writing, painting or other of their passions.

Sadly, we have also had several friends who could not decide what to do about housing and spent their first years of retirement feeling anxious about what they should do. In the end they did nothing, got seriously ill, and died without ever enjoying the retirement they worked their whole lives to get to. Housing in retirement can be a huge issue. Talk with your spouse and decide what is best for you today and in ten or twenty years from now and once you set a goal just take one step at a time until you reach your destination.

In our case, my spouse and I sold our home in the suburbs of Minneapolis, Minnesota and moved to a home we purchased about nine years earlier in the East Valley of Phoenix, Arizona. We left behind one of our three adult children and her family (our only grandchildren), an elderly mother, siblings, nieces and nephews, many friends and previous work colleagues. It wasn't easy but we had decided years earlier that the main priority in determining our location after retirement was to maintain good health for as long as possible. For us, that meant it was essential to find a mild climate where we could walk outside and be active year-round. As we observed our retired and aging relatives and friends who made their homes in the northern climates we noticed how most of them were inactive and tethered to their homes during the cold, snowy winter months. In addition, many of them also became socially isolated during those winter months especially the ones who lived alone. The climate affected them greatly physically, emotionally and mentally, and in our opinion, aged them faster than other people of the same age we met in our development in Arizona. This was a completely unscientific study because we were not aware of the family medical issues or histories of any of the individuals we were observing, nonetheless, it seemed obvious to us that climate made a huge difference in activity and activity made a huge difference in long term health.

At first we thought of keeping two homes and doing the six months *here* and six months *there* routine that appeals to many people in the Midwest and North, but we changed our minds after several years of dual home ownership. The time and money it took to maintain two homes was more than what we wanted to continue spending for shelter in our retirement years (with a fixed retirement income) and also several years earlier, two of our three adult children moved to other parts of the country (even the one in Minnesota, was four and one-half hours away). Once our children were no longer physically located near us, we felt significantly less emotional attachment to the Minneapolis area; it was a nice house but no longer "home" and we made the decision to relocate to Phoenix, Arizona full time and try to use technology to stay in touch. We also travel back to see family and friends as often as possible.

When we first began to research possible retirement locations more than a dozen years ago we made a list of the all the things that were important to us when we retired. If you are considering a move either full or part-time, you may wish to start by making a list of what is most important to you, too. Some of the items on our list included: A Division I University for sports, arts and the availability of college courses, a 55+ active adult community that offered classes, crafts and a well equipped fitness center with a pool and activities as well as a variety of planned social events. A location with no more than a 45 minute drive to a major airport and, the availability of medical facilities, shopping and movies no more than 30-45 minutes away. We found our little corner of paradise about ten years ago in the East Valley of Phoenix. It met all of the criteria we had set and with some sacrifice at that time, we could afford it. It became a seasonal rental while we finished our professional careers and following the sale of our primary residence and subsequent retirement last summer, we moved southwest full time.

We are happy with the choices we made and often say we should pinch ourselves to make sure it is real. Yes, of course, we miss our friends and we would like to be closer to our families, but with air travel, cell phones, email and Skype, we can stay very connected. It may not work for everyone but it does work for us and a lot of other retired people we meet, too. I would credit the success of our move to the planning that went into it ahead of time and being very clear about what we wanted and then creating concrete strategies to reach that goal. If you decide you want to live in a smaller home or a home in a different location, take the time to research locations, set goals and make serious plans to move your dream into reality. If we can do it, so can you.

When retirees sell a home, it requires careful financial planning. Mike Sullivan, Chief Education and Operations Officer for Take Charge America (a non-profit credit counseling and debt management agency) said in a recent interview that there are five questions Baby Boomers should ask themselves when considering such a move.

1. Can we sell our current home and buy another place for less than the amount of money we receive from our current home?

2. Will the costs of our new home be less than the costs of our current home?

3. Will we be happy in the new home (size, location, etc)?

4. If we want to have guests stay with us, will there be room?

5. Can we afford to own two homes at the same time? If not Sullivan suggests that Baby Boomers sell their current home before buying a new one.

Along with the decision to downsize there are many other decisions around choosing a new home, including location (whether to be near adult children, grandchildren and other family or not), climate (sun-belt or skiing), whether to buy in an active adult-only community or a multi-age community, should it be located in a gated or an open community. Do you or your spouse have an elderly parent who depends upon you for current or future care? If you make the decision to sell your long-time family home and relocate, what is the best financial decision; to take out a mortgage or pay cash? Also, are any tax implications on profit from the sale of the previous home? Other financial consideration include making sure that you have enough cash on hand for any purchases or remodeling you wish to do at your new residence and making sure you have enough cash on hand to pay for emergencies that may unexpectedly arise.

When you buy, sell or change homes in retirement there are always trade-offs. Most of the trade-offs are personal choices and should be considered only after a period of reflection, research and planning with your spouse. Not something decided at the spur of the moment or decisions made quickly in the course of a few days. Your retirement years are a time for you to pursue your passions and to thrive; and while every choice has a financial implication, equally important is the opportunity to create the lifestyle you wish to pursue for the next two or three decades of your life. Do your research and make the decisions that meet your needs, be practical and realistic. Be true to yourself. You may want to golf everyday but your budget may only support golfing once a week. If it is important, try to figure out a way to make it happen.

Retirement communities (55+ years or up) are preparing for Boomers and have a lot to offer residents with facilities, activities and social events, visit some before making up your mind one way or another. What is a fantastic fit for one person (or couple) can be pure hell for another. A good way to get the feel of a development is to rent a home for a period of time, get involved with activities and attend social events. If it feels good now, it probably will in the future, too. If it doesn't feel good, you may wish to look elsewhere. Checking out places where a friend or relative has a home (and is happy) is a good idea, too because the transition is easier if you already know someone in the new location. If you haven't lived in an area with a Homeowner Association (HOA) before, this is also a great time to research that aspect of governing body that is created by many retirement developments to maintain facilities, the properties and usually maintain higher home values.

Where to Retire

You can retire to Phoenix, Arizona where...

1. You are willing to park 3 blocks away because you found shade.

2. You've experienced condensation on your hiney from the hot water in the toilet bowl.

3. You can drive for 4 hours in one direction and never leave town.

4. You have over 100 recipes for Mexican food.

5. You know that "dry heat" is comparable to what hits you in the face when you open your oven door.

6. The 4 seasons are: tolerable, hot, really hot, and ARE YOU KIDDING ME?

You can retire to New York City where...

1. You can say "the city" and expect everyone to know you mean Manhattan.

2. You can get into a four-hour argument about how to get from Columbus Circle to Battery Park, but can't find Wisconsin on a map.

3. You think Central Park is "nature."

4. You believe that being able to swear at people in their own language makes you multi-lingual.

5. You've worn out a car horn.

6. You think eye contact is an act of aggression.

You can retire to Minnesota where...

1. You have only four spices: salt, pepper, ketchup and Tabasco.

2. Halloween costumes fit over parkas.

3. You have more than one recipe for casserole (and call it "Hot Dish").

4. Sexy lingerie is anything flannels with less than eight buttons.

5. The four seasons are: winter, still winter, almost winter and construction.

You can retire to the Deep South where...

1. You can rent a movie and buy bait in the same store.

2. "Y'all" is singular and "all Y'al" is plural.

3. "He needed killin" is a valid defense.

4. Everyone has two first names: Billy Bob, Jimmy Bob, Mary Ellen, Betty Jean, Mary Beth, etc.

5. Everything is either "in yonder," "over yonder," or "out yonder." It's important to know the difference, too.

You can retire to Colorado where...

1. You can carry your $3000 mountain bike atop your $500 car.

2. You tell your husband to pick up Granola on his way home so he stops at the day care center.

3. A pass does not involve a football or dating.

4. The top of your head is bald, but you still have a pony tail.

You can retire to the Midwest where...

1. You have never met any celebrities, but the mayor knows your name.

2. Your idea of a traffic jam is ten cars waiting to pass a tractor.

3. You had to switch from "heat" to "AC" on the same day.

4. You end sentences with a preposition: "Where's my coat at?"

5. When asked how your trip was to an exotic place, you say, "It was different!"

You can retire to Florida where...

1. You eat dinner at 3:15 in the afternoon.

2. All purchases include a coupon of some kind—even houses and cars.

3. Everyone can recommend a dermatologist.

4. Road construction never ends anywhere in the state...ever.

5. Cars in front of you often appear to be driven by headless people.

✬✬✬

Getting Organizing

Why be organized? What are the benefits of organizing your belongings, space and time? At times it seems impossible to keep up with all of the demands on our time and as a result our environment and life sometimes fall into a state of chaos. Getting organized goes hand-in-hand with de-cluttering and downsizing and will help you take control of your environment and time.

Some people believe they are simply not capable of being organized and even play the DNA card with statements like "I didn't get the neat gene" or "I know it (office, room, house, car, life) is a mess but it is *my* mess and I know exactly where everything is." Sorry to report it, but the organizers of the world say that is nothing more than an attempt to provide a rationalization to make other people believe there really is a rhyme or reason for the chaos you choose to live in and, by the way, they say *no one* knows what they have or where to find it in complete chaos. Your guess as to the location of any given object is probably no more accurate than would be the guess of a perfect stranger walking in to your mess. That being said, however, the people on the other side of that argument say Einstein and other great thinkers needed clutter and chaos to be creative. Einstein said something to the effect that logic will take you from point A to point B and imagination will take you everywhere. Those who see value in chaos usually add that all the fuss about organization merely takes away ones creativity, spontaneity and fun. The good news is that organizational skills are not connected to DNA and can be learned so you get to choose how you want to live; organized to the *enth* degree or in complete chaos or somewhere in between. Whatever you choose is your right answer.

How do you know if you want or need more organization? If you have ever wasted time rummaging around in piles of stuff searching for things and then in the end possibly given up and purchased an item you already have but could not find, then you may want to consider becoming more organized. Climbing over clutter, being late, missing appointments and forgetting things is a stressful way to live, but you can regain control and feel less stressed through organization. The biggest challenge may be to stop making excuses and get started. Once you sort through all of your belongings and develop an organizational scheme, then the biggest challenge will be to keep the systems in place and knowing that up front can be helpful to your long term success.

You can certainly simplify your life with fewer possessions, a topic discussed in the de-cluttering and downsizing sections, but even if you don't throw anything away you will have more space by just organizing your space. Try it by cleaning out and organizing a drawer or a closet. An added bonus to having order is that it will make it easier to find things quickly when you want or need them. The organizational gurus suggest there are a number of benefits to being organized including the following. You will:

- Have more time for family and friends,

- Be a role model to others, especially the children in your life,

- Manage your calendar, schedule and meet deadlines better,

- Gain respect from others for the way you manage and meet obligations on time,

- Achieve your goals more often,

- Have more time available to engage in healthy activities such as walking and preparing healthy foods,

- Have less stress in your life,

- Sleep better,

- Have less dust in your home and fewer problems with allergies,

- Have more space within your existing space,

- Get energy and peace from your living space,

- Be a happier and healthier person.

This list was compiled from several articles about the value of organizing one's life and while I doubt there is any scientific evidence to support a good number of the benefits identified (perhaps the less dust one), but for the most part the list makes some basic common sense. Nevertheless, organizational skills are not a question of nature vs. nurture and, like everything we learn, it is a matter of education and habit. You must work at learning how to be organized and develop systems to stay that way. Whether your motivation is your health, your pocket book, or something else, time spent organizing your environment and your life, could pay big dividends in peace of mind.

Ask yourself how **you** will benefit from being organized? Make your own list of reasons why you want to become more organized. It may surprise you. And then get going. It is never too late and retirement is a great time, in fact the perfect time, to get organized. There are hundreds of websites devoted to organization that provide hints for everything from setting up linen closets to arranging furniture and managing filing systems. Three sites that offer good ideas and useful articles to help you create an organizing scheme that will make sense to you are:

- http://www.organizeyourself.com

- http://organizedhome.com

- http://www.getorganizednow.com

Remember the key to organization isn't simply the act of placing items neatly in particular places, but making a commitment to put things back after each time using them. It means filing materials immediately; not allowing mail, papers and clutter to pile up. In other words the core truth of organization lies in the old adage: *A place for everything and everything in its place.*

WHAT IT TAKES TO GET TO HEAVEN

After a long illness, a woman died and arrived at the pearly Gates of Heaven. While she was waiting for Saint Peter to greet her, she peeked through the Gates. She saw a beautiful banquet table. Sitting all around were her parents and all the other people she had loved and who had died before her.

They saw her and began calling greetings to her --"Hello" "How are you! We've been waiting for you!" "Good to see you."

When Saint Peter came by, the woman said to him "This is such a wonderful place! How do I get in?"

"You have to spell a word", Saint Peter told her.

"Which word?" the woman asked.

"Love." Said Saint Peter.

The woman correctly spelled "Love" and Saint Peter welcomed her into Heaven.

About six months later, Saint Peter came to the woman and asked her to watch the Gates of Heaven for him that day. While the woman was guarding the Gates of Heaven, her husband arrived. "I'm surprised to see you," the woman said. "How have you been?"

"Oh, I've been doing pretty well since you died," her husband told her. "I married the beautiful young nurse who took care of you while you were ill. And then I won the lottery. I sold the little house you and lived in and bought a big mansion. And my wife and I traveled all around the world. We were on vacation and I went water skiing today. I fell, the ski hit my head, and here I am. How do I get in?"

"You have to spell a word", the woman told him.

"Which word?" her husband asked.

"Czechoslovakia."

✭✭✭

CHAPTER 6

Take Care of Business

Sunday Morning Sex

Upon hearing that her elderly grandfather had just passed away, Katie went straight to her grandparent's house to visit her 95 year-old grandmother and comfort her. When she asked how her grandfather had died, her grandmother replied, "He had a heart attack while we were making love on Sunday morning."

Horrified, Katie told her grandmother two people nearly 100 years old having sex would surely be asking for trouble.

"Oh no, my dear," replied granny. "Many years ago, realizing our advanced age, we figured out the best time to do it was when the church bells would start to ring. It was just the right rhythm. Nice and slow and even. Nothing too strenuous, simply in on the Ding and out on the Dong."

> She paused to wipe away a tear, and continued,
> "He'd still be alive if the ice cream truck hadn't
> come along."

One message that Baby Boomers have heard loud and clear throughout their working years is to save for retirement. While most had set aside some retirement funds, the Great Recession of 2008 raised havoc with their savings and investments as well as the equity value in their homes (which many were counting on for their retirement nest egg). Now a few years later, instead of thinking about a time in their lives when they would not have to set an alarm clock or deal with bosses or customers again, a significant number of Baby Boomers report feeling apprehensive about retirement finances. Moreover many boomers are considering delaying retirement because of the worry that they and/or the system will run out of money during their retirement years.

A fair number of people who have already retired say if they had listened to the news stories telling them they didn't have enough money to retire, they never would have made the decision to retire. Not to downplay the importance of having savings or income beyond Social Security benefits, because it is very important, but more than a few of them also admit they really didn't have a clue as to how much money they would actually need to live in retirement. For most of these retirees it was more of a "learning by doing" experience. The decision to retire came when they were offered a company "buy out" or became eligible for a pension In other words they constructed a retirement lifestyle with whatever amount of money they had at the time of retirement. That being said most claim to be happy with their current lifestyles. Over the years these retirees have found ways to live within their means and, when needed, to supplement their income by taking on small jobs. In retrospect, however, most say they wish they had started with a vision of a retirement lifestyle and then created a financial plan to reach their goals rather than to have let their employer determine when they retired.

One prime example of not having a vision for retirement came from a woman in our development who tells how she and her husband worked hard to prepare for retirement by paying off all of their debts including their mortgage. Even though they had little cash in savings, they felt they could live nicely on two Social Security checks because they didn't have any outstanding debts so when they reached age 62 they both retired. Shortly after retiring her husband died unexpectedly and the woman was left with one very small monthly benefit check which did not meet her monthly expenses. Before long her car broke down and the medical bills arrived for the hospital services her husband had received that were not covered by insurance. This woman was faced with selling her home, her only asset, at about the same time the 2008 Recession hit and the housing market crashed. Fortunately she was able to obtain a reverse mortgage on the house and as a result has been able to provide for herself. She has enough money to live comfortably now but worries about not having an emergency fund and she is saddened that she does not have anything to leave to her son and grandchildren. Was her financial crisis the result of not having a vision (plan) for retirement or not having enough money saved? Very likely it was both but her financial situation today may be more sound if she and her husband had started with a realistic image of the lifestyle they desired and then set aside some money for unexpected emergencies.

Because of this woman's story and others like it, this chapter is not about saving money for retirement *per se*, but rather ideas to help you *"Take Care of* (your) *Business"* in retirement. It is focused on some ways to think about creating a vision for retirement along with a few online tools to help you determine whether your savings goals are on target with your retirement goals. There is also a brief discussion on Social Security benefits, a few words about pensions, recovering lost pensions, credit reports, and some thoughts on Wills, Trusts and digital assets.

Just Wondering

A little old lady was sitting on a park bench in a popular Florida adults-only community.

A man walked over and sat down on the other end of the bench. After a few moments, the woman asked, "Are you a stranger here?"

He replied, "I lived here years ago."

"So, where were you all these years?"

"In prison," he said.

"Why did they put you in prison?"

He looked at her, hung his head and very quietly said, "I killed my wife."

"Oh!" said the woman. "So you're single...?"

✩✩✩

Creating a Vision for Retirement

Taking a line from Steven Covey's book, *The 7 Habits of Highly Successful People*, a good way to plan for retirement is to **begin with the end in mind**. Each person (and couple) needs to figure out what retirement means to him/her/them; and be able to describe it in detail. Too often we are so busy working and making a living that we fail to have a clear picture of what we want in the future. Eventually when that *future* arrives and it isn't all that we had hoped it would be, we accept it with the attitude of "it is what it is." Human nature tends to make the best of what we have and as a result we sometimes settle for something less than what we really wanted, however, it doesn't have to be that way. Part of the problem may be that many individuals are like the people described in the earlier section and simply have no idea what to expect in retirement; no vision. A Senior Vice President at Sun Trust Investment Group, by the name of Joe Sicchitano, was interviewed recently and summed up that same idea when he said, "I can tell you with certainty that 100 percent (of my clients) know what they are retiring *from*; a much smaller percentage know what they are retiring *to*." Think about that for a moment. Do you know anyone like that? Are you clear about what you will retire *to*? Or are you willing to take whatever comes your way?

I have encountered a number of people who are in their first years of retirement are bored and unhappy. They are paralyzed by the idea that they can finally do anything they want and yet they do not have a clue what it is that they want to do. They do not know where or how to begin "living the dream." One friend told me she thought her retirement was more of a nightmare than a dream. This woman and people like her often lack a vision for their lives. Instead they are going through the motions and sleepwalking through their retirement from one day to the next. If you are feeling like that, do yourself a favor and take the time to create a vision for your retirement. Retirement is something most people look forward to for a long time and it is not going to create itself. Well, I suppose it actually will create itself, but it won't be nearly as satisfying of a life for you as it could be if you intentionally designed it. Even if you are currently retired, it is never too late to create or revise a vision for your retirement. You already know how you typically spend your days, so take this opportunity to reconstruct a vision for how you would like them to be rather than how they actually are. Think of it as creating a new blueprint for living.

It seems that having a vision for retirement would be a logical place to start planning for retirement, but a lot of people spend more time planning a vacation than they do their 25 or 30 year retirement. You wouldn't expect to take a vacation without having a few key details in place, such as: knowing your final destination, how you were going to get there, where and how long you are planning to stay and the date you will return home. Moreover, people seldom go on vacation without having some idea of what it is going to cost and how they will pay for it. That being said, why would anyone approach retirement without at least some consideration to those same issues, too? Take the time you need to reflect on the retirement lifestyle that you wish to live then begin by writing down some of your ideas (so that you can begin to build a concrete plan).

A good beginning is to imagine (envision) exactly the kind of lifestyle you desire in retirement. Create a vivid detailed mental picture and include your everyday activities not just the "highlight reel" or "Polaroid" moments. Ask yourself and your spouse some questions to spark your thinking. For example, you may think you want to travel extensively when you retire. Will you travel to faraway national and/or international destinations or short day trips near your home? How often you will travel. Will you travel every day and every month all year long? Or will you make one big trip each year? What will you do when you are not traveling? How do your ideas for travel compare with those of your spouse/significant other and or children and grandchildren? How will you travel? By airplane, car, motorcycle, boat, ship, bike motor home, on foot or another means? Anything is possible; some people who are passionate about travel purchase a motor home or a house boat and live in it while they travel year-round. A number of books, newsletters, travel guides and blogs document that particular carefree Bohemian lifestyle and while it doesn't work for everyone, it does appeal to many people. If traveling is the main focus of your retirement lifestyle, picture it. Make a list of destinations and start collecting travel brochures on them. See yourself engaged in activities when you are visiting those locations.

Perhaps your passion is golf and you cannot wait to retire so you can golf every day. Do you really want to golf *every* day for the next 25 or 30 years? Will you golf alone or with someone else? Do you have a spouse or a close friend to share your dream of golfing? If it is a spouse, is it feasible that you will be able to afford to have both of you golf once, twice or more times a week? Do you live in a climate that supports year-round golf or will you need to consider moving or buying a second home or getting a seasonal rental? Picture yourself golfing. Imagine the golf course you are playing, how you are dressed, your bag of clubs, the cart you are riding on, other people in your group, and your first swing! Bam, a hole in one! Life is good!

Some people take photographs and cut pictures from magazines to create a picture board (collage) representing the activities and the lifestyle they desire in retirement. Having a clear visual representation is very helpful in the goal-setting process. Once you have your ideal retirement lifestyle in mind, the next step toward achieving that way of life will be to figure out approximately how much money it will cost. It may be helpful to write out a daily schedule for a period of three or four weeks. Having an idea of how you will spend your time day-to-day will help you create a more realistic view of your life which in turn will help you to create a more realistic budget and eventually to set more realistic goals. If you are a person who has a desire to create a "Bucket List", this would be a good time to get one started and make sure it becomes part of your retirement vision, too because doing things on a Bucket List cost money, even if it is a one-time event. If you are not a Bucket List person, but perhaps more of a "To Do" or a "Honey Do" kind of person, you may wish to generate a list of home improvement projects you want to complete in the future so that you can factor those costs into your planning, too.

Once you have a vision for an ideal retirement lifestyle and you have completed your daily/weekly/monthly schedule, it is time to work on a monthly budget. Pay attention to detail as you proceed with this step and include travel, hobbies, leisure activities, entertainment, dues and memberships, insurance, etc. as well as the usual fixed costs and day-to-day living expenses (utilities, car, gas and food). When you have completed what you believe could be a typical monthly budget you will want to add special annual expenses such as charitable giving and holiday travel or gifts and calculate a projected annual budget. It isn't going to be an exact budget, but it should give you a general idea of what it might cost to live the retirement lifestyle of your choice.

Service Retirement

The Navy found they had too many officers and decided to offer an early retirement bonus. They promised any officer who volunteered for retirement a bonus of $1,000 for every inch measured in a straight line between any two points in his body. The officer got to choose what those two points would be.

The first officer who accepted asked that he be measured from the top of his head to the tip of his toes. He was measured at six feet and walked out with a bonus of $72,000.

The second officer who accepted was a little smarter and asked to be measured from the tip of his outstretched hands to his toes. He walked out with $96,000.

The third one was a non-commissioned officer, a grizzly old Chief who, when asked where he would like to be measured replied, 'From the tip of my weenie to my testicles.'

It was suggested by the pension man that he might want to reconsider, explaining about the nice big checks the previous two Officers had received. But the old Chief insisted and they decided to go along with him providing the measurement was taken by a Medical Officer.

The Medical Officer arrived and instructed the Chief to "drop 'em," which he did. The medical officer placed the tape measure on the tip of the Chief's weenie and began to work back. "Dear Lord!" he suddenly exclaimed, "Where are your testicles?"

The old Chief calmly replied, " Vietnam. "

✫✫✫

Making a Retirement Plan

Now that you have your ideal retirement lifestyle in mind, and an approximate monthly and annual budget prepared, you are ready to determine the kind of long-term financial plan it will take to live the lifestyle of your dreams? A few more questions to help you summarize what you have done so far and to organize your thoughts as you begin to set long term goals:

- How much money will we need to cover monthly expenses to support the lifestyle we have described?

- Do we have any debts or ongoing expenses that need to be paid off before retirement or that we will have to carry into retirement?

- How much money do we have saved now?

- How much money will we need to save annually to reach our goal?

- Can we do this? Is our budget realistic or do we need to modify the vision?

There are numerous online tools available to help you sort out many variables and to assist you in creating a realistic savings plan. Obviously some calculators are provided by investment firms or advisors whose business is to assist you in making investments so that down the road you will be able to fund your retirement dream AND to make money for them along the way. That last part is not a big secret but not necessarily a bad thing either if you have an agent or firm that you know and trust. When you make money, the sales agent makes money so they may have good motivation to serve you well!

An internet search for goal setting applications will reveal many sites (most are free with no-strings attached). You can use these online tools to obtain ballpark figures of approximately what it will take to finance your future retirement lifestyle. You may wish to start at a site run by the non-profit Employee Benefit Research Institute at **www.choosetosave. org.** If you invest funds through a financial organization, such as the Edward Jones, you can check with your representative for free company planning and goal setting tools. The Edward Jones site, for example, can be found at **www.edwardjones. com/retirementvisionquiz.** Every major investment firm has resources available to current and future customers. These online tools are very valuable in guiding you through various inventories, scenarios and questions that will help you clarify your personal and financial goals. Using tools such as these can simplify the work involved in determining an approximate amount of income you will need to save or invest to support your desired retirement lifestyle in the future.

Other matters that could be considered at this time might include: Are you able to manage your current debt before you retire? Should you hire a financial adviser? Are you prepared for unanticipated emergency expenses that could arise between now and your retirement?

Many financial advisory sites suggest that individuals reduce or eliminate all debt by the time they retire. Every kind of debt including credit cards, mortgage debt, and student loan debt (if you or your spouse has gone back to school in recent years or co-signed for children's student loans). However, if you are very close to retiring, you may not be in a position to eliminate all of your debt so the question may become how much debt you can carry into retirement with the income you expect to have. For most people, the biggest debt expense is a home mortgage or housing costs. An interesting article that addresses the issue of housing in retirement was *recently published in the U.S. News & World Report was titled: "7 Ways to Save on Your Housing Bill in Retirement."* This article was written by Joe Udo (*author of blog* **Retire By 40,**) who asserts that while paying a mortgage can be difficult enough during the working years, it can become an unbearable hardship for many in retirement. He points out that a mortgage payment can easily be as much or more than an entire monthly Social Security check, therefore individuals planning to retire who still have many years left on a mortgage, may have to figure how to reduce their housing costs after retirement. Mr. Udo suggests several options including: paying off the mortgage, renting out spare rooms, downsizing to a smaller home, refinancing your current home (just before you retire), obtaining a reverse mortgage, selling your home and renting instead of owning, or moving in with your kids. Check out the full article in *U. S. News & World Report* or Joe Udo's blog at **Retire By 40.**

This might also be a good time for you to consider the question of whether or not to employ a financial planner/adviser. Your response may depend upon how you feel about your level of expertise in the area of financial planning. Some people know and understand money and investing better than others and so the answer to that question varies by person. Financial planning is a process of setting goals, assessing resources (assets), predicting future financial needs, and developing plans to achieve financial goals. If you have the knowledge and discipline to do that on your own, you may not need outside advice but many people do not have that level of expertise and may wish to consider employing a financial planner. Various elements can be involved in financial planning, including investing, taxes, retirement, and estate planning as well as other services. Financial planning means different things to different people depending upon his/her goals. Many individuals and couples choose to use the services of financial planners to assist them in setting financial priorities and to make decisions that help them work toward long term goals.

That being said, it is important to note that not all financial planners are created equal. Some are certified and some are not, some are paid on commission while others charge a flat hourly fee and each has a different level of education and experience. If you decide that working with a professional financial planner is in your best interest you may wish to ask relatives, friends and colleagues for recommendations. Then spend some time independently researching the individuals whose names you receive before you enter into a business relationship. Ask for references from prospective planners and be sure to talk to the people on the list. In advance of the calls you may wish to identify a few specific questions you want to know and keep notes on the responses. You cannot predict with 100% accuracy that you will select someone who is honest and trustworthy and who will keep your best interests in mind, but if you take the time to do a thorough reference check, you will have a much greater chance of finding the right financial planner who will meet your needs.

Finally, are you prepared for unanticipated expenses? Emergency funds are for those unexpected challenges that can occur at any time during our lives including during our retirement years. There isn't a magic formula for an amount of money to set aside in response to this question, but it still should to be on your radar and part of your retirement planning. The figure I have heard most often is having on hand (liquid and available if needed) an amount of money equal to 6 months worth of living expenses.

Older Men Scam

Women often receive warnings about protecting themselves at the mall and in dark parking lots, etc. This is the first warning I have seen for men. I wanted to pass it on in case you haven't heard about it. A 'heads up' for those men who may be regular customers at Lowe's, Home Depot,

Costco, or even Wal-Mart. This one caught me totally by surprise.

Last month... I became a victim of a clever scam while out shopping. Simply going out to get supplies has turned out to be quite traumatic. Don't be naive enough to think it couldn't happen to you or your friends.

Here's how the scam works; Two nice looking, college-age girls will come over to your car or truck as you are packing your purchases into your vehicle. They both start wiping your windshield with a rag and Windex, with their breasts almost falling out of their skimpy T-shirts. (It's impossible not to look). When you thank them and offer them a tip, they say 'No' but instead ask for a ride to McDonald's.

You agree and they climb into the vehicle. On the way, they start undressing. Then one of them starts crawling all over you, while the other one steals your wallet.

I had my wallet stolen Apr. 4th, 9th, 10th, twice on the 15th, again on the 17th, 20th, 24th, and the 29th. Also May. 1st, 4th, 8th, twice on the 16th &17th, and very likely again this upcoming weekend.

So tell your friends to be careful. What a horrible way to take advantage of us older men. Warn your friends to be vigilant.

By the way, Wal-Mart has wallets on sale for $2.99 each. I found even cheaper ones for $.99 at the Dollar Store.

So please, send this on to all the older men that you know and warn them to be on the lookout for this scam. (The best times are just before lunch and around 4:30 in the afternoon.)

✫✫✫

The Basics of Social Security

As you near retirement age, there are many rights and responsibilities as well as information you need to know about Social Security retirement or survivors benefits. The best source of information for Social Security is always the official government website, **www.socialsecurity.gov.** All of the Social Security programs are accessible at that site and you can set up a personal account with password protection. At the Social Security site you can do all of the following and more:

- Apply for benefits

- Find the address of your closest local Social Security office

- Change your personal information (address, telephone, email)

- Apply for or change a password so you can check your benefits

- Change your direct deposit

- Request a replacement Medicare card

- Ask for letters to confirm benefit amount

- Request copies of publications

- Estimate benefits (before retiring)

The toll-free number of the Social Security Administration is: **1-800-772-1213**. All calls are confidential and the

131

representatives can answer your specific questions from the hours of 7 am to 7 pm, Monday through Friday. There is also an automated response system available 24 hours a day at **1-800-325-0778** where you can update an address or request a replacement Medicare card. To ensure accurate and courteous service a second Social Security service representative monitors some phone calls.

When you work and pay Social Security taxes, you earn credits toward Social Security benefits. If you were born in 1929 or later, you need 40 credits, which are equal to 10 years of full time work at a minimum, to qualify for retirement benefits. The Social Security Administration determines the amount of your benefit by how long you worked and how much you earned. The higher your lifetime earnings, the higher your monthly benefits will be. If there were gaps in your work history or you had low earnings, your benefit amounts may be lower than if you worked consistently or had earned more.

Another factor contributing to the benefit amount is your age at the time you start to receive Social Security. The age referred to as the "full retirement age" is the age at which 100 percent of retirement benefits are payable. You can take early retirement as early as age 62, but if you start collecting benefits before you reach the full retirement age, your monthly benefits will be reduced. There is a benefits calculator on the Social Security website at **www.socialsecurity.gov/retire2/retire-chart.htm** that you can use to determine benefits under various scenarios. If you choose to keep working beyond full retirement to take advantage of a larger payment, your benefit will generally increase by about 7-8 percent per year from the time you reach full retirement age to when you actually start receiving benefits or until you reach age 70.

The decisions about when to retire and to when to begin receiving Social Security benefits are difficult and are dependent upon many individual factors. Do you retire at 62 and have a lifetime benefit of less money for what may be a longer period of time (depending upon how long you and /or your spouse live) or do you wait until a later age and receive higher payments for what may be a shorter period of time (depending upon how long you and /or your spouse live)? Unless you have a foolproof way to predict the future with 100 percent accuracy, at some point you need to lay out the facts, perhaps create a mathematical model, and make a decision. There is an excellent Social Security Administration publication to help you weigh the various factors titled: "When to Start Receiving Retirement Benefits" and it is available at **www.socialsecurity.gov/pubs/10147.html.** You may also wish to use the Retirement Estimator at **socialsecurity.gov/ estimator.**

You can" go green" by using Social Security's online services with no paper, printing, or travel needed. The Social Security Administration has expanded the online services available at **www.socialsecurity.gov/myaccount.** At this secure site you can check your earnings record or estimate future benefits or (if you already receive benefits) check your payment amount, change your address and telephone number in the Social Security Administration records, get a benefits verification letter and change your direct deposit information. You can retire online! It usually takes less than 15 minutes to complete the retirement application at **www.socialsecurity. gov/retireonline.**

A final thought about taxes and Social Security. About one third of those receiving Social Security benefits must pay taxes on some of their Social Security. If your total income, including Social Security and all of your taxable income is $25,000 or more and you file federal taxes as an individual, you will need to pay federal taxes on some of your benefits. For tax year of 2012 the amount is $32,000 for married couples filing a joint return. You will receive a Social Security Benefit Statements (Form SSA-1099) for the tax year by January 31 each year. If you have not received your 1099 by that date, you can request one at **www. socialsecurity.gov/1099.**

The Confession

An elderly man walked into a confessional and the following conversation ensued:

Man: I am 92 years old, have a wonderful wife of 70 years, many children, grandchildren, and great grandchildren. Yesterday I picked up two college girls, hitch-hiking. We went to a motel, where I had sex with each of them three times."

Priest: "Are you sorry for your sins?"

Man: "What sins?"

Priest: "What kind of Catholic are you?"

Man: "I'm Jewish."

Priest: "Then why are you telling me all this?"

Man: "I'm 92 years old...I'm telling everybody!"

✰✰✰

Pensions and Recovering a Lost Pension

If you are one of the millions of Americans who participate in a federal, state government or private pension plan, you already know the importance of keeping track of pension growth and benefits. When you near retirement age it is important to meet with a plan administrator in person. If you are unsure of exactly who to contact or where to go for more information, you might start with the Human Resources Director at your workplace or a union representative (if you are a member of a workers union), or a co-worker who may be more familiar with the pension plan. Generally members nearing retirement age should begin meeting with a plan administrator about five years before they actually plan to retire. This is an opportunity to confirm eligibility and to calculate projected retirement income.

While individuals who are active members of a pension plan usually are well informed about the plan, is not unusual for past workers to lose track of a pension benefit. You may have left employer years ago and simply forgot that you left a pension behind. You may have worked for a company that changed ownership or went bankrupt and you thought the pension was lost, but you may be wrong. There are millions of dollars sitting in pension plans across the United States or with the Pension benefit Guaranty Corporation (PBGC), an agency of the federal government, waiting to be claimed by their lawful owners. According to the PBGC the average unclaimed pension value is approximately $6,500. If you have lost track of a pension there are a number of contacts mentioned later in this chapter to help you search for lost pension money.

If the company you worked for is still in business, contact the human resources department and ask how to contact the pension administrator. Once you get the contact information, simply ask them whether you have a pension, what it is worth and what you need to do to go about claiming it. You can expect

135

to show proof of employment at the company and proof of identity.

Old tax records should have all the information you need but if you no longer have them you can request a copy of your earnings record from the Social Security Administration. Call 1-800-772-1213 and ask for Form SSA-7050, *Request for Social Security Earnings Information*. You can also download the report at **www.SSA.gov/online/ssa-7050.pdf.** Expect to pay a small fee for the report depending on the number of years of data you request.

If your former employer went out of business or if it is still in business but no longer offers a pension plan, check with the PBGC, which guarantees pension payouts to private sector workers if their pension plan fails. It does have a maximum annual limit but nonetheless is worth checking. The PBGC offers an online pension search directory tool at **http://Search.PBGC.gov/mp/mp.aspx** or you can call 1-800-400-7242. The PBGC also has a free publication called *Finding a Lost Pension* which can be requested at www.PBGC.gov/res or by calling 1-800-400-7242.

If your former company has moved, merged or changed owners or changed its name, you may still be able to locate them by contacting the Pension Rights Center which is a non-profit consumer organization in 30 states that offers free counseling and information sessions on pension recovering services. To determine if there is a center near you, check this resource at **www.PensionRights.org** or call 1-888-420-6550. If your lost pension is outside the area served by this organization or if you are trying to locate a federal or military pension, you can contact *Pension Help America* at **www.PensionHelp.org**. This organization may be able to help you by connecting you with various government agencies to assist you in your pension search.

Much of the information on lost pensions provided in the preceding paragraphs came from various articles in several publications but most of them mention or credit an advocate for older Americans by the name of Jim Miller. Jim Miller writes a weekly syndicated information column called "Savvy Senior" that is distributed to more than 400 newspapers nationwide and is considered one of the main sources for pension information as well as other senior citizen issues. In addition to his column Miller also offers a free senior news service at **www.SavvySenior.org.**

Retirement

I watched a dog chase his tail for ten minutes and I was like "wow dogs are easily entertained" and then I realized I just watched a dog chase his tail for ten minutes!

☆☆☆

Free Annual Credit Report

The importance of getting a free annual credit report cannot be over emphasized. In this day and age, each individual must be fully aware of any compromises on his/her credit report. The easiest and best way to do it is to take advantage of the free report at **AnnualCreditReport.com** where each of the three credit bureaus, with no strings attached, will provide a comprehensive report once a year. The three major credit reporting agencies are: Equifax, Experian and TransUnion. Consumers can access reports from all three agencies at one time or a single report from each of the three agencies three separate times during the year a few months apart. Place a credit check reminder on your calendar, right along with birthdays and anniversaries.

Many residents in the retirement community where my husband and I live had a brush with identity theft this past winter. A ring of identity thieves apparently obtained access to consumer credit card information through the online records of a local grocery store chain. Over the course of two months they stole the credit card numbers of more than 450 customers. We had two credit cards compromised as did many of our neighbors and some even had their bank accounts accessed through debit card numbers. It is very frightening to be violated in this way and yet these skilled thieves can gain access to your confidential information and attempt to buy goods on your credit, open new accounts, and add their name to your existing accounts all before you know it is happening. It takes away your peace of mind. The annual credit report is an easy to use and completely free resource available to you to watch your credit.

Additionally, according to the Federal Trade Commission more than one out of five Americans credit reports contain errors. An error can lower your credit scores or make it difficult to obtain loans, qualify for credit or debit cards, be able to rent an apartment, get hired for a job or get a low interest rate on a loan. Errors are difficult to correct in spite of an appeals process because the three major credit reporting agencies usually take the word of your creditors or even collection agencies over the word of the consumer themselves so the sooner you find an error, the sooner you can get it corrected.

An excellent place to learn about resources available to you if you need to correct your credit report is the web site: **SmartCredit.com**. John Ulzheimer, the president of consumer education at this site, has outlined a four-step process to get an error on your credit report corrected:

1. Call the creditor that reported the incorrect information.

2. Follow-up your phone call with a certified letter (return requested) to the creditor reiterating the agreed upon correction.

3. Call the creditor repeatedly until you reach someone who is willing to assist you.

4. Send the credit-reporting agency a certified letter (return requested) disputing the error on your report and asking for the erroneous information to be removed.

Be sure to keep copies of all correspondence and detailed notes of your phone calls identifying the names or employee numbers for each person you speak to and the date and time of each call. If you are unable to get the error removed from your credit report, there is one more process you may use to find a remedy and that is to sue. You can sue the credit reporting agency and/or the creditor in state, federal or small claims court. Small claims court is inexpensive and many people prepare and present their own case in front of a judge whose decision is final. If you want to sue in state or federal court you will want to find a lawyer and a good test of how strong of case you have is to find an attorney who will take your case on a contingency fee which means no money out of your pocket. The attorney takes it for a percentage (often 30-50%) of the amount you win plus a flat hourly rate for time spent (also from the settlement). You probably should not expect to make any money through this process, but your payoff is getting the erroneous information removed from your credit report and restoring your credit rating to a higher level. Obviously if you are unable to find an attorney willing to accept your case on a contingency basis, it may be that in their professional opinion, the case is not strong enough to win. There is a web site that will offer a link to find an attorney at the National Association of Consumer Advocates at **www.NACA.net.**

The Inheritance

When Dan found out he was going to inherit a fortune when his sickly father died, he decided he needed a woman to enjoy it with. So, one evening he went to a singles bar where he spotted the most beautiful woman he had ever seen. Her natural beauty took his breath away.

"I may look like just an ordinary man," he said as he walked up to her, "but in just a week or two, my father will die, and I'll inherit 20 million dollars." Impressed, the woman went home with him that evening and, three days later, she became his stepmother.

✲✲✲

Wills/Trusts/Final Wishes

Living Will

Last night, my wife and I were sitting in the living room and I said to her, "I never want to live in a vegetative state, dependent on some machine and fluids from a bottle. If that ever happens, just pull the plug."

She got up, unplugged the TV and then threw out my beer.

She's such a Bitch!

Federal estate taxes may have become a thing of the past for many people this last year when Congress passed a permanent (whatever *permanent* means to Congress) estate tax exemption ($5.25 million for people who die in 2013 including inflation adjustments for future years), however that does not mean that you can put off or even put aside estate planning altogether. *Take Care of Business* is also a reminder to get your basic legal documents in order. The new federal laws and rules are complex enough as it is but, each state also has their own set of regulations and estate taxes. Currently 14 states and the District of Columbia have much lower exemptions than the federal tax. You may wish to become familiar with the estate tax laws in your state.

Many people review their worth with an estate and tax planning attorney so that upon death, their money and assets go to heirs or those they intended rather than being lost in probate costs and taxes. Often individuals and couples write a Will and/or a Trust for asset protection for their heirs. There are many kinds of trusts including revocable or an irrevocable and a number of hybrids models such as a "Multi-Generational" or a "Bypass Trust." An estate planning attorney explained the basic difference between a Will and a Trust to a group of seniors in a planning seminar recently in the following over-simplified terms:

- If you have a Will, you designate who gets what of your assets and it goes directly to the individuals named. It is like handing over a bag or bags of money to each heir. No strings attached and they can spend it any way they wish whenever they wish. They can spend the entire inheritance right now on a new Lamborghini car if it is enough and they wish to do that.

- A Trust is like "vault" and when you die your assets pass into that vault. They are protected from your heirs' creditors or collectors (if, for example, they are going through bankruptcy) or others are trying to access their money such as a not well liked relative or "in-law." On the other hand your heirs may not have full access to the money either because you determine how much of the inheritance they get annually and all requests beyond that basic amount must go through the approval of a Trustee who is in charge of the assets in the Trust. So in the car example above, if the heir needed a new car and requested extra funding from the Trust for that purpose, the Trustee might say that in the past that person typically drove a Ford, so an amount of money to pay for a comparable Ford vehicle could be withdrawn from the trust but not an amount large enough to buy a Lamborghini.

Whether you want (need) a Will and/or a Trust (living revocable or irrevocable) depends upon many factors unique to each individual such as the size of the estate, if it is a second marriage, if there is a blended family, the desire to provide for future generations, the state of residence at the time of death, the state(s) where property is located and many other considerations that only you and your spouse can decide usually with the help of an estate attorney. In many states, it is legal to write your own Will but obviously that takes a great deal of knowledge and understanding of the legal requirements of your state and many caution about being sure to have the documents properly witnessed and notarized. The attorney who described the difference between a Will and a Trust also said that about 90% of the population plans to write a Will but 75% of that group die without one, so writing your own Will is certainly better than dying without one, but be very clear about what your state does and does not allow if you choose this route. A company with a good reputation and loyal following for will-making software is **www.nolo.com**.

As you embark on estate planning, you may wish to begin by re-evaluating your life insurance if you currently have a policy in place. In the past, life insurance was a popular estate planning tool with either the benefit amount passing to heirs upon the owner's death or the expectation being that the benefit would pay the taxes on the estate. Policies may no longer be needed for those particular purposes being the estate tax exemption is now so high, but it may not be advisable to allow the policies to lapse either. The tax-free benefits that life insurance provides could be valuable income for heirs. The purpose and intent may have changed but certainly should be reviewed with an insurance expert and/or your estate attorney before making any changes or allowing a policy to lapse.

Most resources offering advice on estate planning identify several basic legal documents for each adult person to have in place: A Will, a Living Will, and three Power of Attorney documents (a durable financial power of attorney, a health care power of attorney and a mental health care power of attorney). In each of these documents someone is named to make financial, health-care or mental-health care decisions on behalf of the will-maker (testator) if necessary. Couples may name each other first and then a second and third decision-maker but it is recommended that each person have their own separate documents. A durable financial power of attorney gives the named individual the power to pay your bills and make financial decisions for you if you are unable to make them for yourself. The health care power of attorney gives the named individual the power to make health care decisions except in the case of Alzheimer's, dementia or other mental health issues, which is why you also need to appoint a mental health power of attorney.

In addition to having written instructions in his/her Will, it is very important that the testator has a conversation with the Executor (the person who is named to carry out directions in a will) so that that individual fully understands the will-maker's final wishes. In that conversation the will-maker can describe what is most important with regard to finances, personal possessions and health care directives. It can also be an opportunity to discuss funeral arrangements (music and readings for the service, open/closed casket, cremation, burial place etc.) with the Executor. Individuals who wish to plan and pre-pay their funeral can meet with a funeral Director at any time. Funeral home personnel are very sensitive to your needs and situation and are willing to work with your budget and preferences to create a suitable plan. Individuals can select as many details as they wish right down to what they want served for lunch following the service.

Be clear about whether you wish your decision-maker to follow your directions exactly to the letter of your instructions or whether he/she will have some flexibility. Also make sure that the individual knows where the legal documents are located and if it is in a place that requires a key or code make sure they either have it or know where to find it if needed.. Then tell other people close to you about your final wishes too, so that more than one person knows exactly what you want when the time comes.

A Living Will is a document that describes the kind of health care you wish to receive in the event you are unable to communicate your wishes personally. Once again you will identify a decision-maker (a trusted individual) who will make those decisions on your behalf.

Whether you have substantial assets or not you should have a Will and a Living Will so that your loved ones will have clarity about the division of your property and assets upon your death and your wishes with regard to health care. If there are children under the age of 18, you will also want to designate a guardian in the event both you and your spouse were to die unexpectedly. It is both costly and time consuming for an estate to go through probate plus your heirs will wait months or years before they actually receive their inheritance. While you might decide you need a more extensive and detailed legal estate plan, but at the very least you should have these previously mentioned basic documents to ensure that your assets are properly identified and that important decisions are left to the people you most trust to carry them out and who will protect your best interests.

A few final thoughts on this topic include a reminder to name beneficiaries on all of your financial accounts including brokerage accounts, mutual funds, bank accounts and safety deposit boxes, so that those accounts are not overlooked or lost. Some companies require a separate Transfer on Death (TOD) document to be signed and on file to give heirs an opportunity to continue the accounts rather than having to cash them out at the time of death. Most people keep their stock certificates, insurance policies, birth and marriage certificates, titles, deeds and Social Security cards in a waterproof container in a safe-deposit box or another safe location. Scanning documents and storing information digitally is another option.

It is also advised that you inventory your personal posses-sions including estimated replacement value for estate purposes as well as insurance. In a recent edition of the AARP newslet-ter, a woman from California shared how her parents handled dividing personal possessions among the children and made settling the estate easier for the heirs. The parents made a list of family heirlooms, collectibles and other valuable items such as pictures and furniture. They sent the list to their children and asked each child to mark the items with their interest according to the following three statements:

1. "Really want it"

2. "Would like to have it"

3. "Will take it if no one else wants it"

The adult children each returned the lists to their parents and upon the parents' passing the children found a master inventory of all the items with the name of the child who would receive it among the final papers. It seems like a lovely and fair way to share precious items with loved ones who will continue to cherish them, too. Having an inventory of your belongings will make that process much easier (if you choose to do something like that) as well as also provide valuable information for insurance purposes during your lifetime. If you were to suffer a loss, your insurance company would need to know what you own and have documentation of your belongings through photos or videos. Be sure to include photographs of your home's structure from the exterior and landscaping, too. Keep the photos digitally and/or hard copies in the safe place you store other important papers and documents.

My Next Life

I want to live my next life backwards!

You start out dead and get that out of the way right off the bat.

Then, you wake up in a nursing home feeling better every day.

When you are kicked out of the home for being too healthy, you spend several years enjoying your retirement and collecting benefit checks.

When you start work, you get a gold watch on your first day.

You work 40 years or so, getting younger every day until pretty soon you're too young to work.

So then, you go to high school: play sports, date, drink, and party.

As you get even younger, you become a kid again.

You go to elementary school, play, and have no responsibilities.

In a few years, you become a baby and everyone runs themselves ragged keeping you happy.

You spend your last 9 months floating peacefully in a luxury, spa-like conditions: central heating, room service on tap.

Until finally... you finish off as an orgasm.

I rest my case.

✭✭✭

Digital Assets

One other area to consider in the 21st century is protecting your digital assets and digital estate. Most people have cyber accounts that are accessed only through the Internet and would include brokerage accounts, bank accounts, PayPal balances, online store credits (Amazon.com or EBay for example), and web sites or blogs owned by the deceased as well as digital photo albums, email accounts, social media accounts, collections of downloaded eBooks, digital music and movies. These and other digital assets may have monetary and sentimental value for heirs especially if the web site or blog is revenue generating. Most states do not have laws regarding digital property yet so to protect virtual possessions, we need to create a list and make the information accessible to heirs by listing usernames and passwords and identify how you want them distributed, shared or discarded in you Will and/or in written instructions for your Executor.

Any online accounts also need to be clearly identified in your will, especially if you do not receive printed statements. Take the time to confirm (and follow-up in writing) with the financial institution that the power of attorney will be adequate for your spouse or other designated person to have access to the account if necessary or in the case of your death. If you have recurring bills that are paid online, it is a good idea to provide a list of those and access to your spouse or designated person so that online bill payment will not be overlooked and eventually can be cancelled as your estate is settled.

You may wish to include a revenue-generating blog or web site in your Will so the asset goes to the intended heir who can run it or to be sold as you wish, but be sure to check with the provider service with regard to the transfer of ownership. Many contracts have clauses stipulating what needs to be done in the event of the owner's death. Also list any domain names you own, some may have resale value.

E-mail, social media accounts and photo storage (such as Shutterfly, Costco Photos or Photobin) are the digital story of you and if you do not designate rights or leave a list of user ID's and passwords, they may be lost forever. Few states have laws regarding heir's rights of digital accounts and those that do, vary greatly. If you do not wish to share your account information in advance you may consider at least letting your spouse, a trusted friend or family member know where the list can be found in the event of your death.

If you have extensive digital assets and need help passing them on, there are a number of Internet-based for-fee services that can store and protect your information while you are alive and share it with designated people after your death. Two firms that have built good reputations are SecureSafe **(www.SecureSafe. com)** with prices starting at approximately $15/month or Legacy Locker **(http://LegacyLocker.com)** with an annual subscription of approximately $30/year or $300 for a lifetime subscription.

Chasing Wisdom

An old Doberman started chasing rabbits and before long, discovered that he's lost. Wandering about, he notices a panther heading rapidly in his direction with the intention of having lunch.

The old Doberman thinks, "Oh, oh! I'm in deep shit now!" Noticing some bones on the ground close by, he immediately settles down to chew on the bones with his back to the approaching cat. Just as the panther is about to leap, the old Doberman exclaims loudly, "Boy, that was one

---

delicious panther! I wonder if there are any more around here."

Hearing this, the young panther halts his attack in mid-strike, a look of terror comes over him and he slinks away into the trees.

"Whew!" says the panther, "That was close! That old Doberman nearly had me!"

Meanwhile, a squirrel who had been watching the whole scene from a nearby tree, figures he can put this knowledge to good use and trade it for protection from the panther. So, off he goes. The squirrel soon catches up with the panther, spills the beans, and strikes a deal for himself with the panther.

The young panther is furious at being made a fool of and says, "Here, squirrel, hop on my back and see what's going to happen to that conniving canine!"

Now, the old Doberman sees the panther coming with the squirrel on his back and thinks, "What am I going to do now?," but instead of running, the dog sits down with his back to his attackers, pretending he hasn't seen them yet, and just when they get close enough to hear, the old Doberman says ......"Where's that damn squirrel? I sent him off an hour ago to bring me another panther!"

> **Moral of this story...**
>
> Don't mess with the old dogs... Age and skill will always overcome youth and treachery! Bull Shit and brilliance only come with age and experience.

When you *Take Care of* (your personal) *Business*, you will sleep well at night and enjoy every minute of every day knowing that you have everything planned exactly as you want it to be. Now you can party like it is 1968 without a care in the world!

Disclaimer: A reminder to all readers that all resources listed are those that the author personally found to be helpful but are not endorsing or recommending any of them to you. You are also not being advised or directed to make any personal or financial decisions based upon any information included in this book. Always seek the counsel of licensed professionals for financial and legal matters.

Retirement Activities

I've often been asked, "What do you do now that you are retired?"

Well, I have a chemistry background and one of the things I enjoy most is turning beer, vodka and wine into urine and I'm pretty darn good at it!!!

Thank heaven I paid attention in school!

✡✡✡

CHAPTER 7

Be Happy

The Old Man and the Hunter

An 80 year old man was having his annual checkup and the doctor asked him how he was feeling.

"I've never been better!" he boasted. "I've got an eighteen year old bride who's pregnant and having my child! What do you think about that?"

The doctor considered this for a moment, and then said, "Let me tell you a story. I knew a guy who was an avid hunter. He never missed a season. But one day went out in a bit of a hurry and he accidentally grabbed his umbrella instead of his gun." The doctor continued, "So he was in the woods and suddenly a grizzly bear appeared right in front of him! He raised up his umbrella, pointed it at the bear and squeezed the handle. And do you know what happened?" the doctor queried.

Dumbfounded, the old man replied, "No."

The doctor continued, "The bear dropped dead in front of him!"

"That's impossible!" exclaimed the old man. "Someone else must have shot that bear."

"That's kind of what I am getting at..." replied the doctor.

It has often been said that happiness is the only true measure of personal success. If that statement is true, then what is the key to happiness? Perhaps the answer can be found in the old comic strip "Calvin and Hobbes." It's the one where Calvin described the difference between himself and the rest of the world by saying, "Happiness isn't good enough for me! I demand euphoria!" If Calvin was right each of us must challenge ourselves to live beyond happy through spontaneous and unrestrained enthusiasm!

When a child is born he/she is filled with excitement and curiosity (spontaneous unrestrained enthusiasm) and as a child grows they thirst for fun in everything they do but unfortunately that appetite for seeking joy is often lost by the time most individuals reach adulthood. The realities and responsibilities of life get in the way and looking for fun takes a back seat as we learn to take life far too seriously. As young adults mature, many re-define what happiness (and success) means in terms of how much money they have in the bank, the new car in the garage and a big house full of expensive "toys". When we get to retirement age we realize the big house, car and money are, generally much less important than being happy. Not to say you don't need all of those things to live, you certainly do, but you also recognize that life is short and material possessions are not more important than happiness. The old adage of "you cannot take it with you" rings true and the question becomes how do we go about getting our "fun" back?

This chapter will explore being happy through positivity and gratitude and, if we have trouble sustaining those emotions, then acting *as if* we are happy until we genuinely can feel it.

Listen To Your Mother

A mother was anxiously awaiting her daughter's plane to land. She was returning from a year abroad trying to find adventure.

As the young lady was exiting the plane, her mother noticed a man directly behind her daughter dressed in feathers with exotic markings all over his body and carrying a shrunken head.

When the daughter introduced this young man as her new husband, the mother gasped out loud in disbelief and disappointment and then shrieked, "NO! NO! I told you to marry a RICH Doctor!"

☆☆☆

Positivity

Some of us may need to retrain our thinking to be positive, so *being* positive even when we aren't truly feeling that way is a good place to start. There are many resources available to help us learn (or relearn) positivity including a number of blogs, books, and videos on YouTube and, in fact an entire area of study (Positive Psychology) has evolved from recent research on happiness. One of my favorite blogs is authored by Henrik Edberg, a young Swedish journalist who immerses himself in the task of figuring out how to build a better life through personal development. The blog can be found at **http://www.positivity-blog.com/**. According to Edberg, the Positivity Blog provides "happiness and awesomeness tips that work in real life." Just reading it makes you smile. In addition to inspiring articles this site also offers a number of inexpensive relevant courses, books and various educational materials, too. For example, one recent course was called "How Not to Make a Mountain Out of a Molehill," which includes a discussion about how to **not** add drama or to over-think life's little issues. It regularly features ideas that reinforce common sense and provides good advice for all of us to consider.

PositivelyPositive is another blog about living positive and is dedicated to the principle of Your Attitude + Your Choices = Your Life. It can be found at **http://www.positivelypositive. com**. The home page describes the purpose of this blog: "At its core, Positively Positive is about optimism and inspiration. About seeing the possibility within each person—and within each day gifted us. It's about wisdom and how we lift one another up to richer, more fulfilling lives. It's about tapping into our true nature and capacity."

One more site worth mentioning is Chuck Garrett's blog at *Today; Life is Good* with the "Mission of focusing on and promoting good things that are happening in the world." Garrett recently published a list of the 10 Best Positive Thinking Blogs as voted by positivity devotees in a recent survey:

- **Chief Happiness Officer**

- **Dave Egger's Ted Prize Wish Blog**

- **Hounds Good**

- **Never The Same River Twice**

- **The Daily Mind**

- **The Positivity Blog**

- **Think Positive! Blog**

- **You Already Know This Stuff**

- **You Make It Up!**

- **Zen Habits**

As you can see there are many resources available and dedicated to the topic of developing positivity. More than enough to meet everyone's need. Once you locate one that provides you with positive energy it is easy to sign up for free daily reminders and tips about viewing the world in positive ways.

If you prefer a book to a blog, there are dozens of books about happiness and positivity, too. They can be found easily by searching at any online book seller such as **www.Amazon.com** or **www.barnesandnoble.com.** Books on these topics will help readers understand how the principles happiness and positivity can impact one's life as well as offer strategies to help individuals rediscover fun. Some books are overflowing with common sense; tried and true advice based upon personal experience and others are well documented scientific studies including all the facts and figures to support various happiness hypothesis. Three of my personal favorites are: *Discover the Power of the 3-to-1 Ratio* by Dr. Barbara Fredrickson, *The Happiness Advantage: The Seven Principles of Positive Psychology That Fuel Success and Performance at Work* by Shawn Achor, and *Flourish: A Visionary New Understanding of Happiness and Well-Being by* Martin E.P. Seligman.

In *Discover the Power of the 3-to-1 Ratio*, Dr. Barbara Fredrickson gives the reader tools to create a healthier, more vibrant, and flourishing life. Through her research, she discovered that experiencing positive emotions in a 3-to-1 ratio with negative ones leads people to what she calls a *tipping point,* "beyond which they naturally become more resilient to adversity and effortlessly achieve what they once could only imagine." Dr. Fredrickson further states, "You'll learn to see new possibilities, bounce back from setbacks, connect with others, and become the best version of yourself."

Shawn Achor is a distinguished teacher at Harvard University, where he focuses on positive psychology and through his research in the area of happiness wrote *The Happiness Advantage: The Seven Principles of positive Psychology That Fuel Success and Performance at Work*. Achor has become a leading expert on the connection between happiness and success and in 2012 his research on happiness made the cover of the prestigious *Harvard Business Review*. In addition, Achor's TED talk became one of the most popular of all time with about 4 million views and he has a new lecture airing on PBS called "The Happiness Advantage." Achor is also currently conducting research with the National MS Society to show how medical support can be more effective for those struggling with this particular chronic illness when they are able to sustain a positive attitude over time.

Another work in the area of happiness is *Flourish: A Visionary New Understanding of Happiness and Well-Being by* Martin E.P. Seligman and is best described by an excerpt in the author's own words about the *Original Theory: Authentic Happiness.*

> "Positive psychology, as I intend it, is about what we choose for its own sake. I chose to have a back rub in the Minneapolis airport recently because it made me feel good. I chose the back rub for its own sake, not because it gave my life more meaning or for any other reason. We often choose what makes us feel good, but it is very important to realize that often our choices are not made for the sake of how we will feel. I chose to listen to my six-year-olds excruciating piano recital last night, not because it made me feel good but because it is my parental duty and part of what gives my life meaning."

Being positive can make a huge difference in how happy a person feels and, as the research of the authors previously mentioned and others strongly indicate, there is a high likelihood that being happy may also contribute to how long one lives. Many other books have been written on this topic and a number of resources can be found at various Positive Psychology websites including the following:

- International Positive Psychology Association (IPPA)

- BBC News: The Happiness Formula

- American Psychological Association (APA)

- European Network for Positive Psychology

- National Institute of Mental Health (NIMH)

- Positive Organizational Scholarship at the University of Michigan School of Business

- Positive Psychology Center: Research Information

- Quality of Life Research Center

- VIA Institute on Character

An Adventure While Flying

A man boarded an airplane and took his seat. As he settled in, he glanced up and saw a drop-dead gorgeous woman boarding the plane. He soon realized she was heading straight towards his seat.

As fate would have it; she took the seat right next to him and because he was eager to strike up a conversation he blurted out, 'Business trip or pleasure?'

She turned, smiled and said, 'Business. I'm going to the Annual Nymphomaniacs of America Convention in Boston'

He swallowed hard. Here was the most gorgeous woman he had ever seen sitting next to him, and she was going to a meeting of Nymphomaniacs. Struggling to maintain his composure, he calmly asked, 'What's your business role at this convention?'

'Lecturer,' she responded. 'I use information that I have learned from my personal experiences and research to debunk some of the popular myths about sexuality.'

'Really?' he said. 'And what kind of myths are there?'

'Well,' she explained, 'one popular myth is that African-American men are the well-endowed of all men, when in fact it is the Native American Indian who is most likely to possess that trait. Another popular myth is that Frenchmen are the best lovers, when actually it is men of Jewish descent who are the best. And contrary to popular thought, I have also discovered that the lover with absolutely the best stamina (oddly enough) is the Southern Redneck.'

Suddenly the woman became a little uncomfortable and blushed. 'I'm sorry,' she said, 'I really shouldn't be discussing all of this with you. I don't even know your name.'

'Tonto,' the man said, 'Tonto Goldstein, but my friends call me Bubba.'

Life isn't about waiting for the storm to pass; it's about learning to dance in the rain!

"Very little is needed to make a happy life; it is all within yourself, in your way of thinking." **Marcus Aurelius**

✫✫✫

An Attitude of Gratitude

A first cousin to positivity is gratitude, or perhaps more precisely, an *attitude of gratitude*. Gratitude is well described in the excerpt below by Melody Beattie a young self-help author and blogger.

> "Gratitude unlocks the fullness of life. It turns what we have into enough, and more. It turns denial into acceptance, chaos to order, confusion to clarity. It can turn a meal into a feast, a house into a home, a stranger into a friend. Gratitude makes sense of our past, brings peace for today, and creates a vision for tomorrow." - *Melody Beattie*

It is a beautifully written heartfelt statement that clearly implies that when life gets hectic and chaotic and you are feeling overwhelmed, just take a moment and focus on people and things outside yourself that you are grateful to have in your life. You will soon discover that when you are feeling grateful your feelings will shift from negative to positive. You won't be able to feel angry and grateful at the same time. You won't be able to feel jealous and grateful at the same time. You won't be able to feel hatred and love at the same time.

There has been considerable research in this area and results suggest that grateful people report higher levels of positive states of alertness, enthusiasm, determination, attentiveness and energy. In other words, being grateful to *others* has a positive impact on the way *you* think and feel. You can find a positive emotional state by simply focusing on the parts of your life that you are most thankful for and appreciating the abundance in your life. Happiness gurus such as Tony Robbins or Deepak Chopra say being grateful is an energizing way to start your day and a relaxing way to end it. _Tony Robbins_ suggests you list out all the things you are grateful for as you warm up for your morning exercise. Deepak Chopra has incorporated gratitude exercises into his guided meditations as have many other spiritual leaders.

Thinking about gratitude is something that can easily be pushed to the wayside of our lives when we are busy and generally feeling fulfilled. Sometimes a quick visual reminder can bring you back to a place of thankfulness and gratitude. As I researched this topic, I discovered that many people (like those mentioned previously) identify objects or ways to remind their conscious minds to be grateful. The idea seemed to be helpful so I have listed a few of the visual reminders the experts suggest using:

- **Gratitude Rock.** Find a small rock that feels good to your hand and carry it with you. The idea is when you put your hand in your pocket and touch the rock you will pause and think of someone or something you are grateful for. Even if you forget about it all day long, at least in the morning when you put it in your pocket and in the evening when you take it out, you would be reminded to be grateful.

- **Gratitude Journal.** Every evening date the journal and make a list of things for which you are grateful. In the beginning you may have to bargain with yourself that you have to list at least five separate items, but it will get easier and the lists will get longer.

- **Gratitude Bracelet or Beads.** Having a short string of beads or a bracelet made of beads allows you to give significance to each bead and can be used as a tool to focus on all of the blessings in your life and may lead to meditation and prayer at the end of your day.

- **Mental Map of Gratitude.** Draw a small circle in the center of a sheet of paper and draw lines out from the center to other circles where you have written a description of the people and things you are grateful for in your life. Put it in a place that you will see it daily and add to it.

In the blog titled *The Inner-Power Emails*, Charles Burke offers an exercises he calls the "Gratitude Exercise." For each of 10 days you write down 10 things that you are grateful and happy for in your life. Each item needs to be described in about 50 – 100 words. That's it. It sounds easy enough until you try it, but stick with it anyway. It gets easier. Burke says:

> "Success is a skill. Happiness is a skill. Gratitude is a skill. Like all skills, they must be practiced clumsily before they can be done naturally. So, if you'll devote ten honest days to the practice of feeling true gratitude and happiness, I can promise you a dazzling new skill. A skill that just naturally attracts success like a magnet draws iron. Because nothing attracts good fortune and success like a joyous and grateful heart."

This exercise can help you shift your thinking from the negative to the positive. You will begin to notice more good things happening around you because you know that you have to write 10 things down later so you look for good things. As you begin to view the world around you this way, you are training your brain to focus on the good in your life rather than the negative and as a result, you will feel happier.

Life is all about how we view it and gratitude is one of the most powerful emotions we can experience (by the way, the other one is love). Life is not about what others do to you or the bad things that happen but rather how you perceive the world. Your happiness is in your hands and like Calvin; each of us must challenge ourselves to live beyond happy through spontaneous and unrestrained enthusiasm!

A Sex Therapist

A noted sex therapist realized that people often lied about the frequency of their encounters, so he devised a test to tell for certain how often someone has had sex.

To prove his theory, he filled an auditorium with people, and went down the line, asking each person to smile. Using the size of the person's smile, the therapist was able to guess accurately until he came to the last man in line, an elderly man who was grinning from ear to ear.

"Twice a day," the therapist guessed. But the therapist was surprised when the man said no.

"Once a day, then?" Again the answer was no. "Twice a week?"

"No."

"Twice a month?"

"No."

The man finally said yes when the doctor got to "once a year."

The therapist was angry that his theory wasn't working, and asked the elderly man, "If you only have sex once a year, what the heck are you so happy about?"

The old gentleman answered, "Tonight's the night!"

Husbands

A husband and wife are shopping in their local Wal-Mart. The husband picked up a case of Budweiser and put it in their cart.

"What are you doing?' asked the wife.

"They're on sale, only $20 for 24 cans." He replied.

"Put them back, we can't afford them," demanded the wife, and so they carried on shopping.

A few aisles further the woman picked up a $50 jar of face cream and put it in the basket.

"What do you think you are doing?" asked the husband.

"It's my special face cream. It makes me look beautiful for you," replied the wife.

Her husband retorted: "So does 24 cans of Budweiser and it's half the price!"

He never knew what hit him.

"Let us be grateful to people who make us happy, they are the charming gardeners who make our souls blossom." **Marcel Proust**

✡✡✡

Act "as if"

If you are not used to feeling happy and are struggling with the exercises described in the previous section, a hint to help you overcome this roadblock is to simply act *as if* you are happy. You can trick your brain into believing you are happy while you work on developing new positive thinking habits. Refer back to chapter one on laughing every day, the same principles applies in developing a happy outlook on life. Some of the more common roadblocks to happiness include trying to be perfect, surrounding ourselves with negativity (other people, what we view, what we read), trying to keep up with the *Joneses,* and being stuck in the past or the future,

The first challenge is trying to be perfect. Many people never reach a high level of happiness because they have an image of their perfect life in their mind and reality just doesn't ever quite measure up to that picture. If you are waiting for your life to be television show or movie perfect, you may be focusing and worrying about things that are outside of your control. Consider focusing on the present rather than some fantasy of what might be. Better yet, act *as if* your life is perfect. After all, in whose eyes does it need to be perfect? Only yours, of course, and a good place to start is to identify 10 or more people or things you are grateful for in your life. It will help you to get off the perfectionism band-wagon and remember sometimes good is good enough, so act *as if* you have finally reached perfection.

Surrounding ourselves with negativity is another issue we can control. We don't necessarily do this on purpose, but if you take a step back and think about how you define the world around you (how do you speak to others about life's issues). There may be a negative pattern. For example if we socialize with negative or divisive people, read negative books and magazines, and listen to negative talk shows or news broadcasts that are one-sided and contentious. All of these can have a huge effect on how we think and how we feel. It is nearly impossible to be positive if one is always surrounded with negative. We fall into a kind of thinking that some describe as a "downward spiral" meaning that our day-to-day thoughts and actions build on each other become more and more negative over time until we began to look for the negative side of life and often cannot see the positive even if it is right in front of our nose. For example if someone says it is a beautiful weather today, the person in a downward spiral thinking pattern might say something to the effect that it will probably storm later.

You can always choose to change how you view life by spending more time with positive people or at least changing the topics of discussion to positive topics, reading books that inspire you rather than those that reinforce polarized negative views, fears or hatred. Watch TV shows and movies that make you laugh and think about your life differently than you have before. Reading one of the uplifting blogs previously mentioned is an easy way to start reducing the negative influences in your life. And always, always, ALWAYS assume that other people have positive intentions. There is no way for you to know "why" other people do the things they do, so trying to interpret the intentions of others just adds misery to your own life. Assume the best of everyone and move on.

Another approach to life that can lead to negativity is called *Keeping up with the Joneses*. It happens when people spend too much time comparing themselves to and competing with others. They compare houses, cars, furniture, money, relationships, social popularity, physical looks and more. It is a destructive habit that only leads to a loss of self esteem and reinforced negativity. You can't win if you keep comparing because no matter what you do or how much you have you will always find someone else in the world that has more than you or is better at doing something than you. Just making a conscious effort to realize this is a problem can be a useful beginning to turning this bad habit around. A practical way to deal with this issue is to compare yourself to yourself (see how much you have grown, what you have achieved and what progress you have made towards your goals) and always be kind to yourself and others. Don't define your happiness by what others have.

Spending too much mental energy rethinking about what has happened in the past or dreaming about the future instead of enjoying the present can also rob us of happiness. Our thoughts are like a tape that runs continuously in our minds replaying events that could have been or should have been different; you relive old conflicts or missed opportunities and simply cannot stop thinking about it. It is important to learn from our past and to use that knowledge to plan for the future, but equally important is not to dwell in either place 24/7. If we are not present in life now, we will only miss out on more memories which in turn will anchor you more deeply in fretting about the past and up living with even more regret. To break this habit try making a conscious effort to stay in and savor the present, regardless of what you are doing. Even if it is something as relatively insignificant as reading a newspaper or eating a meal and if you find yourself drifting into an old thought pattern, speak to it. Speak out loud if you are alone and in a place where you can do it, otherwise say it silently to yourself: "Hey, (speaking directly to the negative thoughts) get out of my head; you are not getting my peace of mind today." "You are water under the bridge." "I have moved on from thinking about you." Say whatever you need to make a personal commitment to be fully present wherever you are and in whatever you are doing and to not allow your thoughts to drift to either the past or the future. And, of course, if you can't manage being fully present in the moment right away, act *as if* you are and soon you will be.

"A Minnesota Girl"

Three men were sitting together bragging about how they had given their new wives duties.

The first man had married a woman from Michigan and bragged that he had told his wife she was going to do all the dishes and house cleaning. He said it took a couple days but on the third day he came home to see a clean house and dishes.

The second man had married a woman from Kansas. He bragged that he had given his wife orders that she was to do all the cleaning, dishes, and the cooking. On the first day he didn't see any results, but the next day it was better. By the third day, he saw a clean house, the dishes were done and she had a huge dinner on the table.

The third man had married a Minnesota girl. He boasted that he told her that her duties were to keep the house cleaned, dishes washed, lawn mowed, laundry washed and hot meals on the table for every meal.

He said the first day he didn't see anything, the second day he didn't see anything, but by the third day most of the swelling had gone down and he could see a little out of his left eye, enough to fix a bite to eat, load the dish washer, and telephone a landscaper.

Warning: Beer contains female hormones.

Sydney Un1iversity and CSIRO scientists released the results of a recent analysis that revealed the presence of female hormones in beer.

Men were urged to take a concerned look at their beer consumption.

The theory is that beer contains female hormones (hops contain Phytoestrogens) and that by drinking enough beer, men turn into women.

To test the theory 100 men drank 8 bottles of beer, each within a 1 hour period.

It was then observed that 100% of the test subjects:

- Argued over nothing.

- Refused to apologize when obviously wrong.

- Gained weight.

- Talked excessively without making sense.

- Became overly emotional.

- Couldn't drive.

- Failed to think rationally.

- Had to sit down while urinating.

No further testing was considered necessary.

✿✿✿

Ditch the Emotional Baggage

The State Fair

Morris and his wife Esther went to the state fair every year, and every year Morris would say, 'Esther, I'd like to ride in that helicopter.'

Esther always replied, 'I know Morris, but that helicopter ride is fifty dollars and fifty dollars is fifty dollars'

One year Esther and Morris went to the fair, and Morris said, 'Esther, I'm 85 years old. If I don't ride that helicopter, I might never get another chance.'

To this, Esther replied, 'Morris that helicopter ride is fifty dollars, and fifty dollars is fifty dollars.'

The pilot overheard the couple and said, 'Folks I'll make you a deal. I'll take the both of you for a ride. If you can stay quiet for the entire ride and don't say a word I won't charge you a penny! But if you say one word its fifty dollars.'

Morris and Esther agreed and up they went. The pilot did all kinds of fancy maneuvers, but not a word was heard. He did his daredevil tricks over and over again, and still not a peep. When they finally landed, the pilot turned to Morris and said, 'By golly, I did everything I could to get you to yell out, but you didn't. I'm impressed!'

Morris replied, 'Well, to tell you the truth, I almost said something when Esther fell out, but you know, fifty dollars is fifty dollars!'

Something else that can get in the way of happiness in retirement as well as in the way of building new relationships is what many call "emotional baggage." This is about letting go of past anger and feelings of resentment that some individuals carry around with them like a badge of honor. Most of the time both anger and resentment are absolutely pointless and usually do more harm to the person who harbors the feelings than to the people the feelings are directed toward. Some people carry these negative feelings for years and the intended party may never become aware of that other person's way of thinking.

If you feel like there is a black cloud following you around because you cannot let go of old anger or resentment, you may need some professional help to get past it. A friend of mine was married for 30+ years when she and her husband divorced. Shortly after the divorce he remarried and very soon after that he had a breakthrough idea that made him and his second wife very wealthy. My friend is retired high school teacher who lives very modestly on her pension. She feels hurt and betrayed and is consumed by resentment. Even though we and many other mutual friends have been friends for a long time, no one is allowed to say her ex-husband's name in her presence or even in front of any member of her family for that matter. She claims she isn't able to develop a new relationship because even though she occasionally goes on a date because no man ever calls back for a second one. I can only assume that after spending the first date hearing about how badly she was treated by her previous husband that date is not able to envision a second or third date being much different. Her hatred for her first husband is a huge black cloud hanging over her and it defines her life because that is all she can think about, and as a result of thinking about it continuously, it becomes all she can talk about, too. No one wants to spend the rest of his/her life with someone who is consumed by all that emotional baggage. Prospective suitors probably run away as fast as they can, which only adds to the "woe is me" song being played in this woman's head.

If you feel like you have a black cloud ruining your life, don't waste another precious minute feeling that way. Call your physician for a referral to a mental health professional who can help you and make an appointment as soon as possible. Mark Twain was right on the money when he said, *"Anger is an acid that can do more harm to the vessel in which it is stored than to anything on which it is poured."*

On the other hand if it isn't exactly a full blown black cloud that is following you around, but there is a little static in your attic (your thinking). Perhaps there is someone in your life who knows how to *press your buttons* and spending any amount of time with that individual puts you in a funk for several days. You may need to refrain from seeing him/her all together or if that isn't possible then at the very least, create some strategies to help you process your feelings and get back to living in the present a little more quickly.

A "trick" that I use to reclaim my peace of mind when I get upset about something or someone, is to use a mental image I created awhile back. The image is that of a white *Banker's Box* (the cardboard kind you use to store tax documents or other important papers). I created a mental picture including the fine details of a large, bright white box with a lid. When a problem or a person irritates me (presses my buttons), I picture the Banker's Box and me placing an image of that problem or person into the white box and closing the lid. Every time a thought about the person or issue pops into my head, I say to myself, *"You cannot have my peace of mind today, so into the box you go.*" It is just a little strategy that works for me otherwise I find myself fixating on the issue or person and by the time I have finished over-thinking it, I have usually blown the situation way out of proportion in my mind. In the past that has resulted in me *blowing up* with little or no provocation the next time I saw the person (or encountered the issue). Or sometimes I would *stuff my* feelings deep inside where they would smoulder which then resulted in me feel sad and/or depressed about myself. Neither were positive healthy outcomes so I find that by placing the issue or person into the *Banker's Box*, it keeps it out of my conscious thoughts and generally the whole problem evaporates fairly quickly without causing harm to me or anyone else. I rarely think about what all is in the box, but if I wanted to I could re-create the images of the contents with vivid detail, and retrieve the things I have placed in the box. I could think them through one at a time when I was feeling more calm and logical, but usually a little time lessens the sense of urgency for me and I never bother with retrieving them. If you have some people or issues that are *hot buttons* for you, you may wish to try creating a mental strategy to "store" them until a later time when you are in a better frame of mind to deal with them.

Through a lifetime of people-watching I have also observed that emotional baggage is handled very differently between the two genders. If male friends have a difference of opinion, they may shout at each other, perhaps swear, spit and sometimes even trade blows then walk off in a huff. When the next day rolls around one of them will go over to the other one's place and say, "Want a beer?"

The other replies, "Yeah, you?" They drink beer and never mention the issue again. It is over and done.

Women, on the other hand usually save up what they perceive to be "injustices" until they have enough (emotional baggage) for a "garage sale." They endure insults and injury with a smile on their faces acting as though the little indignations mean nothing. Then one day seemingly out of the "clear blue" a minor rub results in the start of WW III. A woman will scream a litany of abuses, one by one and the list may go back several years or even a decade or more; each incident remembered in great detail and carefully catalogued in the emotional baggage file in their brain carefully connecting one situation to another in a fine spider web of resentment. Having an emotional baggage "garage sale" usually ends the female friendship. However, most women cannot stop there, the next step is to gather a legion of supporters, other women who know the errant party and are willing to publicly agree with the annoyance of the first party. In other words the garage sale game has turned from an individual competition into a team event and mutual friends must take sides. It exacerbates the problem and results in even more emotional baggage being carried around by even more people.

Which brings us to what may be the biggest problem of all for those who actually carry old emotional baggage around and that is no one else (other than a professional who is being paid to do so) cares or wants to listen to you continually spew forth years' worth of the same old gripes against the same old people, things or organizations. Life can be difficult and if you cannot move past the troubles you have encountered on your own, it may be in your best interest to get professional help. For the sake of your happiness, get help sooner rather than later.

More good advice from Mark Twain is to *"Drag your thoughts away from your troubles… by the ears, by the heels, or any other way you can manage it."*

Subject: Car Trouble

Lena's car broke down one day on U.S. 52 just outside of Minot, North Dakota. She eased her car over to the shoulder of the road, got out and opened the trunk. Two men jumped out, Lars and Sven.

They were wearing trench coats and they stood at the back of the vehicle, and faced oncoming traffic. Then they held their coats open and exposed their naked bodies to the drivers who were approaching.

This scene caused one of the worst pileups in history of the highway. It was not long before a police car showed up. The policeman was enraged and ran toward Lena's vehicle yelling, "What is going on here?"

"Ya, vell my car broke down," Lena said calmly.

"Okay, I get that but what are those perverts doing in the back?" asked the cop.

Lena replied, "Vell, officer ... dose are my emergency flashers!"

✯✯✯

CHAPTER 8

Relationships

NO SEX SINCE 1955!!!

A crusty old Marine Sergeant Major found himself at a gala event hosted by a local liberal arts college. There was no shortage of extremely young idealistic liberal ladies in attendance, one of whom approached the Sergeant Major for conversation.

"Excuse me, Sergeant Major, but you seem to be a very serious man. Is something bothering you?"

"Negative, ma'am. Just serious by nature."

The young lady looked at his awards and decorations and said, "It looks like you have seen a lot of action."

"Yes, ma'am, a lot of action."

The young lady, tiring of trying to start up a conversation, said, "You know, you should lighten up a little. Relax and enjoy yourself."

The Sergeant Major just stared at her in his serious manner.

Finally the young lady said, "You know, I hope you don't take this the wrong way, but when was the last time you had sex?"

"1955, ma'am."

"Well, there you are. No wonder you're so serious. You really need to chill out and relax! I mean no sex since 1955! Come with me."

She took his hand and led him to a private room where she proceeded to "relax" him several times.

Afterward, panting for breath, she leaned against his grizzled bare chest and said, "Wow, you sure didn't forget much since 1955."

The Sergeant Major said in his serious voice, after glancing at his watch, "I hope not; it's only 2130 now."

Ya gotta love military time.

As people look forward to retirement they often imagine it will be like finding a magic lamp with a genie who will grant them three wishes. They believe those three wishes will instantly transform their lives to a place of peace and balance with a slower paced life and much less stress to manage as well as being surrounded by positive harmonious relationships. While there may be a kernel of truth in those thoughts, the pace doesn't slow and the stress doesn't disappear overnight by magic and relationships that needed mending before retirement will still need mending after it, too. You create your level of being busy before retirement and you create it after retirement, too. Having a demanding schedule and being on the go isn't unique to those in the work force, many retired people say, "How did I ever have time to work" and others add, "You don't know the meaning of busy until you retire" and a few will even admit to feeling the opposite, "I hate being retired, because I am not busy enough" or "I do not have any structure to my day and I can't live without working toward goals." At the end of the day only you can decide if you are too busy, not busy enough, or just right, and whether you are feeling satisfied and fulfilled with the relationships in your life, or not. None of it will happen by magic. Achieving balance and a peace in your life and relationships will take some time and work (starting with having an idea of what it is you want your life to be like) and it will be well worth the effort in the end.

The Road Trip

While on a road trip, an elderly couple stopped at a roadside restaurant for lunch. After finishing their meal, they left the restaurant, and resumed their trip.

When leaving, the elderly woman unknowingly left her glasses on the table, and she didn't miss them until they had been driving about forty minutes.

By then, to add to the aggravation, they had to travel quite a distance further before they could find a place to turn around, in order to return to the restaurant to retrieve her glasses.

All the way back, the elderly husband became the classic grouchy old man. He fussed and complained, and scolded his wife relentlessly during the entire return drive. The more he chided her, the more agitated he became. He just wouldn't let up for a minute.

To her relief, they finally arrived at the restaurant. And as the woman got out of the car, and hurried inside to retrieve her glasses, the old geezer yelled to her, 'While you're in there, you might as well get my hat and the credit card, too.'

"Age is an issue of mind over matter. If you don't mind, it doesn't matter." **Mark Twain**

✼✼✼

Love and Marriage in Retirement

Wise Old Woman

Sally was driving home from a business trip in Northern Arizona when she saw an elderly woman walking on the side of the road. As the trip was a long and quiet one, she stopped the car and asked the old woman if she would like a ride. With a silent nod of thanks, the woman got into the car.

Resuming the journey, Sally tried in vain to make a bit of small talk with the old woman, but the old woman just sat silently, looking intently at everything she saw, studying every little detail, until she noticed a brown bag on the seat next to Sally.

"What's in bag?" asked the old woman.

Sally looked down at the brown bag and said, "It's a bottle of wine. I got it for my husband."

The old woman was silent for another moment or two. Then speaking with the quiet wisdom of an elder, she said: "Good trade....."

THE HUSBAND STORE

A store that sells husbands has just opened in New York City, where a woman may go to choose a husband. Among the instructions at the entrance is a description of how the store operates.

"You may visit the store ONLY ONCE! There are six floors and the attributes of the men increase as the shopper ascends the flights. There is, however, a catch: you may choose any man from a particular floor, or you may choose to go up a floor, but you cannot go back down except to exit the building!"

So, a woman goes to the Husband Store to find a husband.

On the first floor the sign on the door reads:

Floor 1 - These men have jobs

Moving on to the second floor the sign reads:

Floor 2 - These men have jobs and love kids.

She decided to move on to the third floor where the sign reads:

Floor 3 - These men have jobs, love kids, and are extremely good looking.

"Wow," she thinks, but feels compelled to keep going.

She goes to the fourth floor and the sign reads:

Floor 4 - These men have jobs, love kids, are drop-dead good looking and help with the housework.

"Oh, mercy me!" she exclaims, "I can hardly stand it!"

Still, she goes to the fifth floor and sign reads:

Floor 5 - These men have jobs, love kids, are drop-dead gorgeous, help with the housework, and have a strong romantic streak.

She is so tempted to stay, but she goes to the sixth floor and the sign reads:

Floor 6 - You are visitor 31,456,013 to this floor. There are no men on this floor. This floor exists solely as proof that women are impossible to please.

Thank you for shopping at the Husband Store.

TV

One night an old married couple was at home watching TV. The husband had the remote and was switching back and forth between a fishing channel and the adult channel.

The wife became more and more annoyed and finally said: "For god's sake! Leave it on the adult channel. You already know how to fish!"

One evening my spouse and I were enjoying a dinner party with a group that included one couple who had been retired for many years, several couples nearing retirement and the two of us (enjoying our first year of retirement). The topic of conversation in many gatherings such as this one is often the same (how retirement changes your life) because for those nearing retirement it seems like a members-only club with a secret handshake and they want the keys to the clubhouse door early. Being the newest to retire, we were asked, "What has been the best part your retirement so far?" My husband answered by saying for him the best part was that *I* was no longer working and under so much stress and tension as I had been in my previous job. I was sorry that he felt that way, but, wow, how lucky am I?

My response was that the growth of our relationship was the best part of the first year of retirement. I went on to add that although we have always felt like we had a strong marriage and, we are committed to each other for the long haul of the whole better or worse deal, there were times over the years that we have bickered a little or occasionally sniped at each other. Neither of us liked how that felt at the time but we didn't talk about it either. We just moved past it and got on with living, but retirement has changed that dynamic. We have moved our relationship full circle and are back to being playful and loving like we were in the first years of our marriage. Retirement has been an opportunity for us to reconnect and spend more time with each other and as a result, I believe our marriage has grown stronger than ever. The long time retired couple hosting the party agreed that the growth in their relationship was the best part of retirement for them, too, and they have been married for 60+ years.

In our case, my husband and I can actually laugh at ourselves now whereas when we were working (and stressed out at times), we might have responded to teasing differently. A few evenings ago we were in a discussion about a movie star and I made some off-the-wall comment, to which my husband jokingly responded, "Really, you thought that? What rock have you been living under?" In the last 15 or so years I might have taken offense and challenged that remark with some indignation, but not last night. I could see the humor in my not knowing something that was as obvious as the nose on my face so I pointed at a large rock in our yard and said, "That one right there!" We both laughed, no affront was taken by either of us and neither got upset or went to bed mad. My point is that relationships ebb and flow as couples go through the phases and challenges of life and, if you wish to have a healthy long-term relationship; retirement is a great time to recapture some of the sizzle and spark in your marriage. One place to begin is through communication and you can start by having long, open, honest non-judgmental discussions as often as possible.

In my opinion, communication is the most important ingredient for maintaining a healthy marriage relationship anytime but especially during retirement. Not the kind of communication that is just general run-of-the-mill discussions about household chores and "to do" lists, but rather deep exchanges of ideas about goals and dreams as well as light playful interactions that can result in the two of you sharing inside jokes and laughter together. Even if you have been talking about goals and dreams for years and you don't feel like there is anything new to add, talk about it anyway. You may be surprised where it will take you. Talk about books you like to read, an activity you enjoy or a movie you want to see. Don't assume just because you live under the same roof together that he/she knows all about you and can read your mind. When my husband and I moved to Arizona we agreed to walk to a local convenience store every morning to buy a newspaper rather than have it delivered. We do love our news so every morning bright and early we walk down the street and it is a perfect time to talk with each other and set the tone for the day. Now we have graduated to having serious talks at other times and other places, too.

Talk with your spouse about everything and don't forget to include conflict resolution. Conflicts arise at every stage of life including the retired years so it is best not avoid it, but rather practice how to approach disagreements on little things so that when bigger problems arise, you won't resort to negative reactions like yelling, walking away, getting mad or giving the other person the silent treatment. Find ways for each of you to calm yourself and talk about your feelings and the issues like two loving adults. Relationship experts say that one of the benefits of a long marriage is that most couples argue much less than in the early years because they learn how to handle disputes and how to live with disagreement and/or compromise on some topics. If you are looking for help in this area, a couple of resources recommended on this topic include:

- Mary Lou Galician's (Dr. Fun) web site: **http://www. public.asu.edu/~drfun/**

- The love Team Game Plan (Richard and Dede Brown: **www.loveteamgameplan.com.**

"Love Team" is a great name for a couple and speaking of communicating **and** love, it is also very important to express your love for your spouse every day. Face it, life is busy and can be demanding even in the retirement years and we assume the important people in our lives know we love them. William Shakespeare said, "They do not love, that do not show their love." Many wives/husbands feel taken for granted because it has been such a long time since they have actually heard the other one say the words, "I love you." Most couples haven't fallen out of love but rather have fallen out of the habit of expressing their love for each other. Try to think and act like you did when you were courting.

The happiest couples I know in retirement take the time to make a gesture of love every day. It can be a very simple statement like "I love you" or "Thank you for .... (fill-in-the-blank), you are a wonderful (thoughtful, great, fantastic) husband or wife." You may feel a little weird saying things like this at first (especially if it has been a while) and it may take

188

some time before it feels completely comfortable Sometimes it is easier to put your feelings into writing so mix it up a little by adding a few hand written love notes here and there too. Using humor also breaks the ice. When my husband does something nice or says something funny that makes me laugh, I like to say, "And that is why you are the love of my life." While you are at it, try adding an unexpected touch, a hug or kiss along with a statement of love; it is like winning the lottery for both people. Knowing you are loved keeps your world filled with peace and happiness.

Even in retirement, it can be hard for couples to find time to spend with each other so another strategy to help keep your relationship strong is to go on a date night regularly. Relationship experts say that we all "chase" love and often after we find it, the "chase" is over and frequently the relationship grows stagnant. A stagnant relationship can happen to couples who have been married only a few years as well as those who have been together for decades. Some say children provide the common thread that keeps couples close and while that may be true, when they grow up and leave home it may become easier for couples to grow apart and create separate interests and lives. A date night allows couples to reconnect and rekindle the "chase." Make a commitment to date night by buying tickets in advance or making a reservation and writing it down on the calendar so you will not schedule something else during the same time or have an excuse to back out altogether. It is advised to have a date night at a minimum of one time per month. Remember to share in the responsibility of date night and be creative by having one spouse plan the date night one month and the other spouse the next. Try new things, too; do not opt for a pizza, beer and a movie every time!

✡✡✡

Togetherness

A relationship difficulty some newly retired couples face is too much togetherness. Retirement can create a new dynamic for couples because you may suddenly have much more face time with your spouse than you did when you were both working and it can create challenges for your marriage. Togetherness is usually not an issue for couples who have spent their whole married life working together in a family business. They already know how to manage "together" and "alone" time; it is old news to them in retirement. However, couples who are accustomed to both individuals working away from home (8-10-12 or more hours a day) and who have developed a routine of interacting together for a few hours in the evenings and on weekends, it is difficult to plunge into a situation where you are with each exclusively other every minute of every day and night 24/7/365. Some spouses feel smothered and as though they have suddenly lost their own personal identity.

Relationship experts say while it is important to nurture your relationship as a couple and to have friends and interests together, it is equally important is for each partner to develop his or her own individual talents, hobbies, interests, and friends too. It keeps you feeling vibrant as a person and as a result you will be more vibrant as a partner. The best place to start, once again, is with an open discussion with your spouse where you talk about expectations and boundaries and follow-up by each of you pursuing some of your own interests, too.

✲✲✲

Money

Another significant topic for retired couples to address together is money. It is important to talk about money issues regularly so both partners are well informed about the family finances. Over time, most couples usually develop a division-of-labor that generally results in one person taking over the financial responsibilities such as paying bills, banking, investing and paying taxes which leave the other partner not knowing as much about the finances as perhaps he/she should. There are many horror stories about the family "money manager" dying first and the remaining spouse scrambling to locate and understand the finances under the worst of all possible conditions.

Retirement is a perfect time to make sure that both spouses fully know and understand the family finances including cash, assets, savings, investments, taxes etc. Being retired often means a fixed income, but there are still bills and taxes to pay so if both spouses have not been involved managing finances in the past, there isn't a better time than the present to start. You may wish to begin with some low-stress kinds of money conversations before tackling the more serious ones.

Even with feeling a sense of urgency, some people simply do not want to get involved with finances---just give me a checkbook and leave me alone kind of attitude---but regardless of how you feel about managing money, talking with your spouse about money matters and making financial decisions together now can save you both much anxiety in the future. At the very least, a monthly finances meeting with the money manager spouse updating the non-money manager spouse on all current aspects of the family financial picture is advisable.

✲✲✲

Party like its 1968

Another topic worth mentioning in the realm of retirement relationships is socializing. Retired people (especially those who reside in retirement developments) have a lot of social gatherings and attend a lot of parties that are usually a mix of both married couples and singles. Most married people act like they are married and interact with others accordingly, no problem. However, every now and then you will find yourself in a group where it seems there are a few individuals who are married but try to act like they are single or perhaps more accurately they act like they want to be single again and they flirt with others there. By this time in life nearly everyone knows that a flirting partner can be a relationship killer and it rarely has good outcomes for a married person. If you or your spouse likes to flirt, it may seem innocent enough to you and could even be how you have always approached social events. However, this is a different time in your life and there are people who are lonely and looking for a partner, so they may take your actions seriously. Therefore you may want to think about your behavior and consider acting another way in social gatherings before it becomes a problem for your marriage. Divorce in retirement seems like an odd phenomenon (if you stuck it out this long why would you split now...) but many retired couples are torn apart by divorce during a time that could be some of their best years together and often it starts with something as foolish as flirting.

Remember the grass isn't greener on the other side of the fence; the grass is green wherever you water it! If you want to keep your marriage intact, then act like it is the most important thing in your life! Flirt with your spouse; it will add romance and help keep your marriage from becoming boring. It never hurts to be spontaneous and plan surprises to rekindle your passion, excitement and sexual arousal for each other. Make love often (no kids at home, no job, the dog won't care); in fact try having sex in the morning or the afternoon; mix it up a little from your usual routines, its great!

Lessons the happiest couples share about love and marriage in retirement:

- **Take the time every day to show your spouse you love him or her.** Say you are sorry, buy a gift, write a note, stop what you are doing and really focus on listening to them when they speak.

- **Do not be critical of your spouse.** Do not belittle, be condescending or argumentative. Instead be understanding and offer your spouse love and compassion. It is not your job to judge them. Agree to disagree.

- **People are more important than things, problems or projects.** It is more important to love your spouse than to be right in an argument.

- **Do not get distracted by things that are not important.** Life is busy and it is easy to get lost in any number of things that will consume your time, but keep your best self focused on your spouse. Remind yourself your marriage matters.

- **Have fun together.** Step up your efforts to look for things that will bring joy to your spouse even if it isn't something you might be crazy about doing. Then allow yourself to let go and enjoy it.

Married and Waiting

An elderly man at a marriage seminar was asked how long he had been married. He said he was married for almost 50 years.

"Wow," the leader gushed, "that's amazing, perhaps you can take a few minutes to share how you stay married to the same woman for so long."

"Well," he said after thinking for a few moments, "I try to treat my wife well, buy her presents and take her on trips. For our 25th anniversary I took her to Tahiti."

What a beautiful philosophy and a true inspiration for all of us," the leader said, ""maybe you can tell us what you are going to do for your 50th anniversary."

"Well," he said, "I'm thinking of going back to Tahiti to pick her up."

Guys' Rules

At last a guy has taken the time to write this all down. We always hear "the rules" from the female side, now here are the rules from the male side of the story on how to keep a relationship strong. Please note... these are all numbered "1" ON PURPOSE!

1. Learn to work the toilet seat. You're a big girl. If it's up, put it down. We need it up, you need it down. You don't hear us complaining about you leaving it down.

1. Sunday sports. It's like the full moon or the changing of the tides. Let it be.

1. Shopping is NOT a sport. And no, we are never going to think of it that way.

1. Crying is blackmail.

1. Ask for what you want. Let us be clear on this one. Subtle hints do not work! Strong hints do not work! Obvious hints do not work! Just say it!

1. Yes and No are perfectly acceptable answers to almost every question.

1. Come to us with a problem only if you want help solving it. That's what we do. Sympathy is what your girlfriends are for.

1. A headache that lasts for 17 months is a problem; see a doctor.

1. Anything we said 6 months ago is inadmissible in an argument. In fact, all comments become null and void after 7 days.

1. If you won't dress like the Victoria's Secret girls, don't expect us to act like soap opera guys.

1. If something we said can be interpreted two ways and one of the ways makes you sad or angry, we meant the other one.

1. You can either ask us to do something or tell us how you want it done, not both. If you already know best how to do it, just do it yourself.

1. Whenever possible, please say whatever you have to say during commercials.

1. Christopher Columbus did not need directions and neither do we.

1. ALL men see in only 16 colors, like Windows default settings. Peach, for example, is a fruit, not a color. Pumpkin is also a fruit. We have no idea what mauve is.

1. If it itches, it will be scratched; we do that.

1. If we ask what is wrong and you say "nothing," we will act like nothing's wrong. We know you are lying, but it is just not worth the hassle.

1. If you ask a question you don't want an answer to, expect an answer you don't want to hear.

1. When we have to go somewhere, absolutely anything you wear is fine...Really.

1. Don't ask us what we're thinking about unless you are prepared to discuss such topics as baseball, the shotgun formation, or monster trucks.

1. You have enough clothes.

1. You have too many shoes.

1. I am in shape; round is a shape.

1. Thank you for reading this. Yes, I know, I have to sleep on the couch tonight; but did you know men really don't mind that? It's like camping.

✿✿✿

Dating in Retirement

Senior Dating

Dorothy and Edna, two senior widows, are talking.

Dorothy: "That nice George Johnson asked me out for a date. I know you went out with him last week, and I wanted to talk with you about him before I give him my answer."

Edna: "Well, I'll tell you. He shows up at my apartment punctually at 7 P.M., dressed like such a gentleman in a fine suit, and he brings me such beautiful flowers! Then he takes me downstairs, and what's there but a luxury car ... a limousine, uniformed chauffeur and all. Then he takes me out for dinner ... A marvelous dinner ... Lobster, champagne, dessert, and after-dinner drinks. Then we go see a show. Let me tell you, Dorothy, I enjoyed it so much I could have just died from pleasure!"

"So then we are coming back to my apartment and he turns into an ANIMAL. Completely crazy, he tears off my expensive new dress and has his way with me two times!"

Dorothy: "Goodness gracious! So you are telling me I shouldn't go out with him?"

> Edna: "No, no, no ... I'm just saying, wear an old dress."

After many years of marriage a number of retirees lose a spouse to death or divorce and find that they are single once again. Someone said I should also add *death by golf* to the list, but I don't think that would be reason enough to start dating again. If it was, one of the other two categories would surely apply before too long. Some people are self-sufficient and have a good network of family and friends and do not need or wish to pursue another relationship and others are lonely without a partner and feel out of place and alone even if they are out in a group.

The prospect of dating after being married a number of years can be very intimidating for a lot of people. Everyone knows, at least in theory, that you can meet someone new through friends, family or organizations such as a church group or those connected to a professional organization, a club or hobby. There are also the less appealing choices of going to a bar or hanging around the produce section at the local supermarket (said to be the number one place to meet someone new and to secure a date) which sounds absurd to most of us as well as a pretty chilly way to spend an evening. And then there is the online option which sounds oddly curious to many Baby Boomers. However, it seems to be the way to meet someone new these days and with an abundance of Websites advertising matches for those over 40 it may be a viable option for many. What is a person to do?

There are a few fears to overcome when dating the second time around as well as several precautions if you decide to try an online match-making option. First, there is the fear of being considered unattractive or too old to interest anyone else. You may feel like you need a style update. If you do feel that way, you may consider asking a close friend to help you or meeting with a style consultant at your favorite department store. Generally speaking you should keep in mind that the people who may be your prospective dates will have aged over the years, as well, and hopefully are in a place in their lives where they feel there is more to meeting someone than his or her physical appearance. Good health and vitality are always attractive at any age and so are self confidence, having a variety of interests and being able to carry on a conversation.

Another fear, if one chooses an online option and posts a profile, is that no one will be interested. I has been said that the 50+ segment of this market is the fastest growing age group on dating Web sites so that prospect is highly unlikely. Some online services are free but most require a fee for the time you wish to have an active profile. Because so many single seniors have been successful in finding partners through online sites numerous publications have offered tips in using this venue successfully. A few cautions or tips that are commonly repeated from article to article include keeping the following ideas in mind if you create an online profile:

- Don't belabor your life story (write a relatively short profile),

- Don't submit badly out-dated photos,

- Don't include photos of yourself with members of the opposite sex,

- If you are family oriented, don't feel that you cannot mention children or grandchildren, just do it generically not by name to protect their safety, and do not post photos of children or grandchildren,

- Do not provide your home address, phone number or home email address (set up an email account and or voice mail account just for this purpose),

- Don't assume you are in a relationship just because an email exchange has gone well,

- Don't discuss prior marriages or relationships on a first date (some say not on the second either),

- Don't assume that online dating won't work for you because of a bad first date with one person or that you do not do particularly well in expressing yourself in email.

There are dating Web sites that are considered *mainstream* as well as those that are highly personalized *niche* sites. There are niche sites that are designed to appeal to nearly every special group you can think of: Christians, pet owners, active fit people, Jewish singles, Catholic singles, Lutheran singles, people over 50 years old, people over 60 years old, people over 70 years old vegans, etc. etc. etc. If you feel strongly about something and wish to date someone with that same or a similar passion you may wish to locate a niche site that caters to individuals with those same interests and likes.

ULTIMATE FEMALE JOKE

A woman was sitting at a bar enjoying an after work cocktail with her girlfriends when Steven, a tall, exceptionally handsome, extremely sexy, middle-aged man entered. He was so striking that the woman could not take her eyes off him.

The young-at-heart man noticed her overly attentive stare and walked directly toward her (as all men will do). Before she could offer her apologies for staring so rudely, he leaned over and whispered to her, 'I'll do anything, absolutely anything, that you want me to do, no matter how kinky, for $20.00....on one condition.'

Flabbergasted, the woman asked what the condition was. The man replied, 'You have to tell me what you want me to do in just three words.'

The woman considered his proposition for a moment, and then slowly removed a $20 bill from her purse, which she pressed into the man's hand along with her address. She looked deeply into his eyes, and slowly and meaningfully said....

'Clean my house.'

Medical distinction between Guts and Balls

We've all heard about people having Guts or Balls. But do you really know the difference between them?

There is a medical distinction between Guts and Balls. In an effort to keep you informed, here are the **definitions**:

GUTS - Is arriving home late after a night out with the boys, being met by your wife with a broom, and having the Guts to ask: **"Are you still cleaning, or are you flying somewhere?"**

BALLS - Is coming home late after a night out with the guys, smelling of perfume and beer, lipstick on your collar, slapping your wife on the butt and having the Balls to say: **"You're next, Chubby."**

I hope this clears up any confusion on the definitions and by the way ….**Medically speaking there is no difference in the outcome.**

☆☆☆

CHAPTER 9

Everything Else

There is so more that could be shared about the first year(s) of retirement, but sooner or later this book has to come to an end. I am missing the old people's swim time down at the watering hole (pool) so this final section will include a few thoughts on a few (mostly unrelated) subjects that deserve mention because they are frequently the center of conversations with other retirees on a regular basis and they include: encore careers, having a Bucket List, volunteering, and revisiting some classic books you may not have read since high school.

The Parrot....

A woman was thinking about finding a pet to help keep her company at home. She decided she would like to find a beautiful parrot. It would not be as much work as a dog, and it would be fun to hear it speak.

She went to a pet shop and immediately spotted a large beautiful parrot. There was a sign on the cage that said $50.00.

"Why so little," she asked the pet store owner.

The owner looked at her and said, "Look, I should tell you first that this bird used to live in a whorehouse and sometimes it says some pretty vulgar stuff."

The woman thought about this, but decided she had to have the bird anyway. She took it home and hung the bird's cage up in her living room and waited for it to say something. The bird looked around the room, then at her, and said, "New house, new madam."

At first, the woman was a bit shocked at the implication, but then thought, "that's not so bad."

When her two teenage daughters returned home from school the bird saw them and said, "New house, new madam, new whores."

The girls and the woman were a bit offended at first, but then began to laugh about the situation.

A few minutes later, the woman's husband, Keith, came home from work. The bird looked at him and said, "Hi, Keith".

Encore Careers

Many Baby Boomers view retirement as a time to sleep in, play golf and to tackle projects around the house or yard that have been put off for years. Retirement is a good time to "work" at all of those things, but some people simply cannot afford to stop working when they reach retirement age and continue to hold a full or part-time job for financial reasons. Other people rejoin the workforce after retirement because they wish to use this time in their lives to pursue a particular passion or to make a difference in the world not because they need extra income. Whatever the reason, many people choose to accomplish their goals by pursuing a second career after retirement. The term that has been coined to describe this second calling is *encore career.* As the number of Baby Boomers moving into retirement continues to grow and the concept of encore careers becomes increasingly popular there is getting to be quite a number of books and guides on this topic. Like with any popular subject, there are as many opinions about to approach an encore career as there are people willing to write a book on the topic, but they all seem to agree on one thing: Retirees who rejoin the workforce after retirement, have a lot more going for them than they realize, but they still should expect that they will need to update their skills in one area or another. Several useful books that focus on preparing retirees for encore careers that could be a good place to explore a new start, include the following:

- *Encore Career Handbook: How to make a living and a difference in the second half of life* by Marci Alboher.

- *Generation Reinvention* by Brent Green.

- *Power Years* by Ken Dychtwald and Daniel Kadlec,

- *Great Jobs for Everyone 50+: Finding Work That keeps You Happy and Healthy…And Pays the Bills* by Kerry Hannon, and

- *The New Frugality: How to Consume Less, Save More, and Live Better* by Chris Farrell

In addition to books aimed at a self-directed approach to preparing for an encore career, many universities have devoted staff and resources to assist retired adults who wish to re-enter the workforce, too. Assistance is available for those wishing to volunteer in their past careers as well as those wishing to acquire additional skills to enter a completely new field and everything in between. Several of the books mentioned above have guidelines and procedures to help retirees create resumes' or prepare for job interviews. Alboher's book, for includes many tips to make sure individuals are making the right career match for themselves before they invest a huge amount of time or money in preparing for a job they ultimately may not want. It also has suggestions for a successful transition and how to know when the time is right to make a move to a new job.

If you are looking for an encore career is to help make financial ends meet, then you may want to start with Chris Farrell's *The New Frugality: How to Consume Less, Save More, and Live Better*. If you are ready to identify what you want from a second career and whether it needs to provide some income for you, this book is a good place to start. On the other hand, if you are just beginning your thought process and are to the point where you say to yourself that a new career has to be something meaningful and will help to make the world a better place, Kerry Hannon's *Great Jobs for Everyone 50+: Finding Work That Keeps You Happy and Healthy…And Pays the Bills* is a good book to launch your journey. It contains valuable information about finding financial as well as personal and professional satisfaction in a second career, and like the others listed, it is jam-packed with practical advice.

The retirees, featured in the research in the books mentioned in this chapter, indicate feeling a very high level of satisfaction once they were established in an encore career and while they described many challenges along the way, all agreed it was an adventure of a lifetime and they would recommend it to others without reservation.

My 1st day of employment

After landing my new job as a Wal-Mart greeter, a good find for many retirees, I lasted less than a day......

About two hours into my first day on the job a very loud, unattractive, mean-acting woman walked into the store with her two kids, yelling obscenities at them all the way through the entrance.

As I had been instructed, I said pleasantly, 'Good morning and welcome to Wal-Mart. Nice children you have there. Are they twins?'

The ugly woman stopped yelling long enough to say, 'Hell no, they ain't twins. The oldest one's 9, and the other one's 7. Why the hell would you think they're twins? Are you blind, or just stupid?'

So I replied, "I'm neither blind nor stupid, Ma'am, I just couldn't believe someone slept with you twice.

Have a good day and thank you for shopping at Wal-Mart."

My supervisor suggested that I probably wasn't cut out for this line of work.

✫✫✫

Creating a Bucket List

An Emergency

An elderly Floridian called 911 on her cell phone to report that her car has been broken into and she was crying hysterically as she explained her situation to the dispatcher:

"They've stolen the stereo, the steering wheel, the brake pedal and even the accelerator!" she cried.

The dispatcher said, "Stay calm. An officer is on the way."

A few minutes later, the officer radios in. "Disregard." he says. "She got into the back-seat by mistake."

The 2007 the hit comedy movie, *The Bucket List,* inspired millions of people to think about their lives in a different way, prioritizing what is important and identifying their deepest desires by creating their own personal Bucket Lists. The main characters in the movie produced a list of things they wanted to do and places they wanted to see before they died (kicked the bucket). Since that movie Bucket Lists have become very popular especially among the retired who have the time and money to make their dreams come true. Many of our retired friends travel extensively, sky dive, take dance lessons, and go on hot air balloon rides and everything imaginable in between. They are living lives without regret by having a Bucket List and planning for and enjoying once-in-a-lifetime experiences one at a time.

My spouse and I have spent this first year of our retirement reinventing ourselves; getting relocated, refreshing our home, getting our affairs in order, establishing healthy exercise routines, building a circle of friends and making many of the decisions and taking many of the actions outlined in this book. We have made lists but mostly of the "to-do" kind with things like replacing the washer and dryer, fixing the door, painting the living room, adding plants to the yard, and so forth. Now, a year later, we are feeling settled and organized and are at a place in our lives that we are ready to make a list of places to travel and things we want to do. I am not sure we will call it a *Bucket List* (meaning that we have a burning passion about completing each item on the list before we *kick the bucket*) but we will have fun making a short list, prioritizing it and doing some of the things on it. Our list will be low key and aligned with our retirement motto which is: If it causes stress, or requires us to stand in line, dress up or it feels like work; it ain't gonna happen!

When you search the term "Bucket List" you will find many sites that offer an enormous number of Bucket list ideas; as many as 75,000 or more for you to consider for your bucket list. Wow! The thought of 75,000 ideas is too much for me to think about but some people find it helpful and can use it to spark a few ideas of their own. Creating a bucket list should not feel like work or be one more thing to do or cause you any stress. Certainly you should not write a bucket list simply because others are doing it. Yes, there is peer pressure even in retirement. However, if you are the kind of person who likes to work toward goals or you want to add some fun, inspiration and enthusiasm into your life, you may want to consider creating a Bucket List.

Nursing Home Care

A man goes to visit his 85-year-old grandpa in the nursing home.

"How are you feeling grandpa?" he asks.

"Feeling fine," says the old man.

"What's the food like?"

"Terrific, wonderful menus."

"And the nursing?"

"Just couldn't be better. These young nurses really take care of you."

"What about sleeping? Do you sleep okay?"

"Absolutely, no problem! At 10 o'clock they bring me a cup of hot chocolate and a Viagra and that is it. I go out like a light for nine or ten hours solid every night."

The grandson is puzzled and a little alarmed by this so he rushes off to question the nurse in charge.

"What are you people doing," he says, "I am told that you are giving an 85-year-old Viagra on a daily basis. Surely that can't be true?"

"Oh, yes," replies the head nurse. "Every night at 10 o'clock we give him a cup of hot chocolate and a Viagra tablet. It works wonderfully well. The hot chocolate makes him sleep like a baby, and the Viagra stops him from rolling out of bed!"

✬✬✬

Stay Busy and Volunteer

If you do not wish to pursue a second career or hold a job after you retire, but you still want to make a difference. Don't forget to volunteer your time and talent and share your treasure. Volunteer opportunities abound around us so check with a local church, food shelf, fraternal organization, county, school etc. You will be able to find a match for your talents and your interests. "The best way to cheer yourself up is to try to cheer somebody else up." **Mark Twain.**

The Raging River

Three men were hiking through a forest when they came upon a large raging violent river. Needing to get on the other side, the first man prayed, "God, please give me the strength to cross the river."

Poof! God gave him big arms and strong legs and he was able to swim across in about 2 hours, having almost drowned twice.

After witnessing that, the second man prayed, "God, please give me strength and the tools to cross the river."

Poof! God gave him a rowboat and strong arms and strong legs and he was able to row across in about an hour after almost capsizing once.

Seeing what happened to the first two men, the third man prayed, "God, please give me the strength, the tools and the intelligence to cross the river.

Poof! God turned him into a woman. She checked the map, hiked one hundred yards up stream and walked across the bridge.

✫✫✫

Books You Haven't Read
Since High School

Some of the greatest literary works ever written are read primarily by high school students who may be too young to fully understand or appreciate them. A retired friend and neighbor recently told me he had always intended to re-read some of the classics when he had time in his retirement years and now that he is retired he decided against it because he "knows how they end." That is not a good excuse, there is so much more to them than how they end. You may truly enjoy rereading some books you haven't read since high school. How you view them as an adult and your depth of understanding may surprise you.

A great place to start may be with some of Mark Twain's popular books like *The Adventures of Huckleberry Finn* and *The Adventures of Tom Sawyer*. Others that have also been recommended include: *To Kill a Mockingbird, The Age of Innocence, Catcher in the Rye, Pride and Prejudice, The Great Gatsby, A Separate Peace, Animal Farm* and *Gone with the Wind*. This list covers a variety of topics, time periods and genres. If you have a little extra time on your hands, a luxury many of us haven't known in years, it could be a great opportunity to pick up some of these books (or other classics) once again. Mysteries and romance novels are fun, but don't forget to challenge yourself with a classic from time to time, too. It is great exercise for your brain.

The Story of Me

One day, long, long ago, there lived a woman (That would be me....) who did not whine, nag or bitch.

But that was a long time ago and it was just that one day.

✩✩✩

CHAPTER 10

The End

After 40 years of marriage...

A married couple in their early 60s was celebrating their 40th wedding anniversary in a quiet, romantic little restaurant. When suddenly, a tiny yet beautiful fairy appeared on their table.

She said, 'For being such an exemplary married couple and for being so loving toward each other for all this time, I will grant you each a wish.'

The wife answered, 'Oh, I want to travel around the world with my darling husband.'

The fairy waved her magic wand and - poof! – Two tickets for the Queen Mary II appeared in her hands.

The husband thought for a moment: 'Well, this is all very romantic, but an opportunity like this will never come again. I'm sorry my love, but my wish is to have a wife 30 years younger than me.'

The wife, and the fairy, were deeply disappointed, but a wish is a wish!

So the fairy waved her magic wand and poof... the husband became 92 years old.

The moral of this story: Men who are ungrateful bastards should remember that fairies are female .....

Dear Readers,

I don't have all the answers. I don't even have all of the questions. Isn't that why we have daytime television? My husband and I danced merrily into retirement thinking we were **R-E-A-D-Y** (the bold capital letters kind of ready) for retirement. Then much to our amazement we were bombarded with information (some real and some not), bombarded with change (some wanted and some not) and bombarded with decisions (some we knew how to make and some we did not). We found out weren't ready for everything that came our way and I suspect you won't be either, but perhaps you have found one or two ideas in this book that will make your transition to retirement a little bit easier

My husband and I are lucky to have a "village" of friends and neighbours who help us make sense of what we do not understand and, of course we solve many problems together (a good number of them over Happy Hour) which can't be all bad. We have a plan to stay active and as healthy as possible for as long as possible and we have our legal house in order (which, gives us great peace of mind and allows us to concentrate on having even more fun). We take life one day at a time and stay busy but at the same time we make a point to live in the present moment so as not miss a single adventure. I think we have made it to where every day is like Saturday which is a good thing.

We are enjoying an incredibly happy retirement and ....
oh, yes, remember Rule # 1 and Rule # 2 at the beginning of
the book? We have developed a few more *rules* for life over the
course of the year; in fact we live by about a dozen that are tailored to meet our needs. These are our rules:

1. Laugh every day.

2. Do not forget Rule #1.

3. Do not set an alarm clock (get up when you wake up---
    unless you want to roll over and get up later).

4. Do not stand in line for anything (unless the President
    of the United States or the Queen of England visits, and
    even then it is only a 50-50 chance at best).

5. Do not dress up (except for weddings and funerals).

6. Walk and exercise every day.

7. Get out and shake a tail feather (dance) at every oppor-
    tunity available.

8. Don't take things so seriously, laugh at yourself.

9. Always remember that your spouse is the love of your
    life (treat accordingly).

10. Stay in touch with family and close friends (you never
    know when you may need a loan).

11. Stay busy, idle time can be the root of evil at any age.

12. If it isn't fun, don't do it!

It is time to close this chapter (book) on our first year of retirement. Holy Sh**, Sherlock! It's year two, what happens now? I wish you a long, happy and healthy retirement filled with more laughs, joy and wonder than you can imagine!

Disclaimer: A reminder to all readers that all resources listed are those that the author personally found to be helpful but are not endorsing or recommending any of them to you. You are also not being advised or directed to make any personal or financial decisions based upon any information included in this book.

Getting Old

At a nursing home in Florida, a group of senior citizens were sitting around talking about their aches and pains. My arms are so weak I can hardly lift this cup of coffee," said one.

"I know what you mean. My cataracts are so bad I can't even see my coffee," replied another.

"I can't turn my head because of the arthritis in my neck," said a third, to which several nodded weakly in agreement.

"My blood pressure pills make me dizzy," another contributed.

"I guess that's the price we pay for getting old," winced an old man as he slowly shook his head. Then there was a short moment of silence.

> "Well, it's not that bad," said one woman cheer-
> fully. "Thank God we can all still drive."

"Against the assault of laughter nothing can stand." **Mark Twain**

✵✵✵

References

Achor, Shawn. *The Happiness Advantage: The Seven Principles of Positive Psychology That Fuel Success and Performance at Work.* New York: Broadway, 2010. Print.

Alboher, Marci. *The Encore Career Handbook: How to Make a Living and a Difference in the Second Half of Life.* New York: Workman Pub., 2013. Print.

"AnnualCreditReport.Com." Web. 28 July 2013. <http://www.annual-creditreportcom.com/>.

"Are You Ready For A Unique Laughter Yoga Wellness Experience?" *American School Of Laughter Yoga.* July 2013. Web. 18 Oct. 2013. <http://www.laughteryogaamerica.com/>.

"Arizona State University." Dr. Mary-Lou Galician, Web. 28 Apr. 2013. <http://www.public.asu.edu/>.

"The Benefits of Exercise." *Mayo Clinic.* Mayo Foundation for Medical Education and Research, June 2013. Web. 1 June 2013. <http://www.mayoclinic.com/health/medical/HomePage>.

Berry, Jennifer Ford. *Organize Now!: A Week-by-week Guide to Simplify Your Space and Your Life!* Cincinnati, OH: North Light, 2008. Print.

Buettner, Dan. *Blue Zones Nine Lessons for Living Longer From the People Who Have Lived the Longest.* Second ed. Washington, DC: National Geographic Society, 2008, 2012. Print.

Burke, Charles. "The Inner Power Emails." *Life With Confidence.* Web. 28 Mar. 2013. <http://www.life-with-confidence.com/>.

"Calorie Counter." *Free , Diet & Exercise Journal.* Web. July 2013. <http://www.myfitnesspal.com/>.

"Clean House, Cut Clutter, Get Organized at Home!" *Organized Home.* Web. 28 July 2013. <http://organized-home.com/>.

"Competitive, Straightforward Pricing." *Merrill Edge.* Web. May 2013. <http://offers.merrilledge.com/simplepricing/>.

Covey, Stephen R. *Living the 7 Habits: Stories of Courage and Inspiration.* New York: Simon & Schuster, 1999. Print.

Department of Health and Human Services, Office for Civil Rights. Web. Feb. 2013. <http://www.hhs.gov/ocr>.

Dychtwald, Ken, and Daniel J. Kadlec. *The Power Years: A User's Guide to the Rest of Your Life.* Hoboken, NJ: John Wiley & Sons, 2005. Print.

"Edward Jones: Making Sense of Investing." *Edward Jones: Making Sense of Investing.* Jan. 2013. Web. 21 Apr. 2013. <http://www.edwardjones.com/retirementvisionquiz.>.

Farrell, Chris. *The New Frugality: How to Consume Less, save More, and Live Better.* New York: Bloomsbury, 2010. Print.

"Federal Trade Commission Protecting America's Consumers." *Federal Trade Commission*. Web. Jan. 2013. <http://ftc.gov/>.

"Free Diet Plans at SparkPeople." *SparkPeople*. Web. Jan.-Feb. 2013. <http://www.sparkpeople.com/>.

Green, Brent. *Generation Reinvention: How Boomers Today Are Changing Business, Marketing, Aging and the Future*. New York: IUniverse, 2010. Print.

Hannon, Kerry. *Great Jobs for Everyone 50+: Finding Work That Keeps You Happy and Healthy...And Pays the Bills*. Hoboken, NJ: John Wiley & Sons, 2012. Print.

"How to Prepare for Retirement." *Choose to Save*. July 2013. Web. July 2013. <http://choosetosave.org/>.

"John Ulzheimer | SmartCredit Blog." *SmartCredit Blog RSS*. Web. 21 July 2013. <http://www.smartcredit.com/blog/tag/john-ulzheimer/>.

"Laughter Is the Best Medicine." *HELPGUIDE*. 1 Dec. 2012. Web. 14 Dec. 2012. <www.helpguide.org>.

"Lawyers, Legal Forms, Law Books & Software, Free Legal Information - Nolo.com." *Nolo.com*. Web. 28 Feb. 2013. <http://www.nolo.com/>.

"Legacy Locker - Return Home." *Legacy Locker*. Web. May 2013. <http://legacylocker.com/>.

"The LoveTeam Game Plan." Web. 28 July 2013. <http://www.loveteamgameplan.com/>.

"Medicare.gov." : *The Official U.S. Government Site for Medicare.* Web. Apr.-May 2013. <http://www.medicare.gov/>.

Miller, Jim. *Savvy Senior.* Jan. 2013. Web. May 2013. <www.Savvy Senior.org.>.

National Association of Consumer Advocates. Web. 3 June 2013. <www.NACA.net>.

"Organize Yourself Online - An Easy-To-Use Service to Help You Get Your Life Organized." Web. 28 July 2013. <http://www.organizeyourself.com/>.

Pension Help America. Pension Rights Center, Washington, DC, Jan. 2013. Web. Mar. 2013. <https://www.pensionhelp.org/>.

Pension Rights Center. Pension Rights Center, Washington, DC, Jan. 2013. Web. Jan. 2013. <http://www.pensionrights.org/>.

The Secrets of Centenarians (2010): *U.S. Census Bureau.* Evercare by United Healthcare, Mar. 2013. Web. <www.Evercare100at100.com.>.

"Secrets to Living Longer." Interview by Katie Couric. ABC News, 9 Apr. 2013. Web. <http://news.yahoo.com/blogs/katies-take-abc-news/secrets-living-longer-145037327.html>.

"SecureSafe." *Swiss Online Storage – Secure Online Storage.* Web. May 2013. <http://www.securesafe.com/>.

Seligman, Martin E. P. *Flourish: A Visionary New Understanding of Happiness and Well-being.* New York: Free, 2011. Print.

"Simpler Daily Work: 13 Smart Habits That Will Help You." *The Positivity Blog*. Henrik Edberg, Web. 28 July 2013. <http://www.positivityblog.com/.>.

"Social Security." *The United States Administration*. Web. Apr.-May 2013. <http://www.socialsecurity.gov/>.

Sullivan, Mike. "Overview of Services." *Take Charge America*. Web. June 2013. <http://www.takechargeamerica.org/services/>.

Udo, Joe. "7 Ways to Reduce Housing Bills in Retirement." *Retire By 40 RSS*. U S News & World Report, 2 May 2013. Web. May 2013. <http://retireby40.org/about-2/>.

"What Is FatSecret?" *All Things Food and Diet*. Web. Mar.-Apr. 2013. <http://www.fatsecret.com/>.

"What Is Laughter Yoga?" *Laughter Yoga International*. No. 33, Galaxy Enclave, Jakkur Plantation, Jakkur, Bangalore India, Dec. 2012. Web. 21 Feb. 2013. <http://www.laughteryoga.org/english>.

Www.PensionRights.org. Web. 7 Jan. 2013. <http://www.PensionRights.org>.

"Your Attitude + Your Choices = Your Life." *Positively Positive*. Web. July 2013. <http://www.positivelypositive.com/about/>.

✧✧✧

About the Author

B.A. Ginther grew up in a small town in the upper Midwest. She spent 38 years in the field of education as a dedicated social studies teacher, Staff Development Coordinator, Quality Compensation Coordinator, Interim Executive Director of Teaching and Learning and a self-proclaimed Director of Fun at a high achieving suburban district near Minneapolis, Minnesota. While her work in each of those areas was noteworthy and often met with acclaim and various honors, her real passion was (and is) to make people laugh. B.A. Ginther lives happily ever after with her husband in a retirement community in Gold Canyon, AZ where she has found a new audience for her old jokes (or is that an old audience for her new jokes)…. Whatever!

One of B. A. Ginther's favorite quotes is: **Live your life in such a way that every single morning when your feet hit the floor Satan shudders and says, "Oh shit, she's awake!"** Although the author is unknown Ginther believes it could have been her mother or her husband; because it describes her approach to each day so perfectly. Who knew? You can email the author at bg667911@gmail.com.

Made in the USA
Lexington, KY
16 February 2014